THE UNPEOPLED SEASON

A Journal of Solitude and Wilderness

Daniel J. Rice

This book is dedicated to my old neighbors
many of whom I sensed but never saw
may you always be illusive
and stay forever wild.

Wilderness Camp

June 12 - October 8, 2011

Note from the author

To preserve the integrity of this pristine landscape, I have selected not to mention it by name, though I am certain someone familiar with the area, or even a resourceful stranger, can ascertain the location based on the details in this book. I only ask that if you acquire this information, and if you ever visit this wild and majestic land, that you treat it with the same tenderness and respect you would provide your own child. For that's what wilderness is, the world in its infancy. It is a separate world where all of our original wonder still exists. It can be, and more importantly, must be, preserved.

*There is a passage to happiness. It's through
an unmarked pathway in the dark forest.
Tangled like your dreams. It waits
for you with open eyes…*

June 12, 2011 Saturday

Today I arrived home for the first time. Today all the dreaming and planning and *what-ifs* became real. Today I am an unemployed writer living as a recluse in the great Northwoods.

The planning for this adventure began a year and a half ago, in central Wyoming, while sitting beside a campfire, beneath a moonlit sky, in proximity to a mountainous trout stream, when Mayana and I wondered *what-if* we both resigned from our jobs and moved into the great outdoors. At the time, Mayana and I had known each other for less than six months, and we lived together in a small yellow house in Casper, Wyoming. She was working as a Senior Planner for an engineering firm — an accomplished position for a person in their early thirties. I was working as a Hydrologic Technician for the United States Geological Survey, which meant I spent much of my time snowshoeing into remote mountain locations or hiking across desert-like high plains, to stand waist deep in a river and record streamflow measurements and collect surface water samples. We spent most of our free time divided between hanging out with friends, and traveling to scenic areas around the wild and untamed state of Wyoming. When it came to spending time in nature, we never could get enough.

Our favorite recreation was camping beside a trout stream high in the mountains. Mayana would spend the day hiking with her camera, or relaxing with a book, while I'd put on my waders and take my fly rod to the river in pursuit of the next trout. Trout. That single word may just mean a fish to many people, but to me, and perhaps other anglers of the fly, that single word conjures images of winding rivers and cobblestones that nobody's eyes but my own have ever seen. Trout. No matter how many of them I catch, they forever remain elusive.

We each pursued our own activity until the sun began to fall, and then we would rendezvous at camp, and spend the night conversing beside a fire while enjoying a couple of drinks, and listening to the sound of darkness. Life was easy and enjoyable, and we could have lived like that forever. But there was something more, some phantasmal possibility lingering over our thoughts, calling us to another place. A world deeper than these recreations.

The dream of a wilderness, and living as the ancients did, that was the life we wanted.

We sat up one night, in a place so distanced from civilization, that no matter how loud we talked or howled, no ears could hear us — save for the mountain lions, rattlesnakes, elk, and coyotes. We watched the moon move across a vast nocturnal sky, and we considered our options. We knew we were not alone in this quest — returning to nature has been a dream present in the minds of every generation since humankind first left nature. This made it simultaneously powerful and sacred. Powerful because we felt to be part of a historical back-to-the-land movement. Sacred because we knew it simply wasn't possible for everyone who wanted that life.

Since I am currently writing this journal with a #2 pencil, and I must sharpen it with my knife after several sentences, I'm going to attempt brevity. Long story short, and several drinks later, we decided to purchase a piece of property in northern Minnesota, where prices were more affordable than land in Wyoming, and the landscapes were pristine. We would live frugally and save money for one year, and then resign from our careers in Wyoming, sell most of our possessions, and spend an entire summer and autumn living in our own private wilderness. We would need enough money saved to maintain land loan payments, purchase grocery supplies while living in the woods, and have adequate money remaining afterwards to live off of while we found new jobs and moved back into civilization.

For the following year we lived frugal. Cut ties with friends so we wouldn't be tempted by social activities.

Reduced our weekly grocery allowance by half. Didn't eat from restaurants. New clothes came from thrift stores or garage sales, and books from the library.

Thanks to a strict regimen of frugality, within a year we owned fifteen acres of forested land, with 350 feet of river frontage, in north-central Minnesota, about fifty miles south of Canada. This is where I am today, sitting in a small clearing in the thick forest, beside my bags of camping supplies. When we first traveled here to purchase the property, we spent the night camped beside the river, listening to wolves howling after dark. In the morning, there was a fresh pile of bear scat between where we had camped, and the two-track driveway where the Jeep was parked. We had discovered a land suitable for this adventure.

Back in Wyoming, several months before our scheduled departure from our civilized lives, and our anticipated arrival to our wild ones, Mayana made a revision to the plan. She was hesitant about transitioning into a lifestyle of financial insecurity. She took a new job as the City Planner for Bemidji, Minnesota, a quaint little culture-rich town about an hour and a half drive from our property. In the spring of 2011, we purchased a house near the southern shore of Lake Bemidji. This is where Mayana would live while I was at camp. She would spend her weekends visiting me in the wild.

Now here I am, living in the forest alone. This fact both invigorates me, and plagues me with uncertainty. What am I going to do with my time? I could spend many hours with my fly rod pursuing the muskie in this river. I could study guidebooks and become a master naturalist. I could sit on a log beside the river in long ruminations about the meaning of existence.

Or, I could write a novel. This journal is not my novel. In fact, I have no intention of ever publishing it. But it does act as an easy release of my thoughts since there is no one here to hear me but my dog, Sly.

I have started several novels in the past couple of years, but have never gotten more than a hundred pages written before becoming distracted by real life. You know what that is, the nine to five (or rather, for me, the six to six) workday followed by just enough energy upon returning home to take care of a few mandatory chores before resorting to the couch with either a television controller or a book in hand. I needed a break from that life. I knew in the forest there would be no distractions, save for my own wandering thoughts. But aren't wandering thoughts the greatest device of a novelist? So I have an obtainable goal: I will live alone in the wild and complete my first novel.

As I get comfortable here with my first day on our property, I look around at my new reality with a feeling that it is too good to be real. I think about the life I left behind and hope that I made the right decision. What if after this adventure I am unable to find a good job? The economy is in recession and people much more qualified than myself cannot find work. But I will risk it. I must risk it, or else I will never know. Not knowing would be worse than failing. It might be worse than anything.

I shake these thoughts from my head. Regardless of what the future may hold, I have an opportunity to spend the next several months living alone in this forest. Even if the life of a poor man awaits me, I will have no regrets, for today I am living my dream.

It's getting dark out now. Sly, a ten-year-old Siberian husky, has fallen asleep beside my feet. I better set up my three-man dome tent and start a fire. Tomorrow I will retrieve the rest of my supplies from the trailer and begin to set up camp.

...

I completed the setup of my tent, and have been sitting by the fire for several hours. I had cut a good supply of firewood, but am down to the last couple of logs. I was hoping to hear wolves howl tonight, but so far, they have been silent. Perhaps they are creeping through the darkness.

June 13 Monday

I spent most of the day retrieving supplies from the trailer and hauling them to camp. It's approximately four-hundred feet of overgrown forest from camp to where the Jeep and trailer are parked, and another eight-hundred feet from camp to the river's edge. The Jeep is parked on an overgrown two-track driveway about a half mile from the nearest county road. My cell phone doesn't acquire reception until I get about fifty feet from the road, and as I walked there earlier to call Mayana, I saw many deer tracks and the furry scat of a timber wolf.

The location I have selected for camp is a natural clearing on a small hill. Within this clearing are ten tall aspen trees, and the perimeter is surrounded by a thick wall of balsam fir. The floor of this clearing is carpeted with wild grasses and firm top soil, and decorated with columbine, wild sarsaparilla, bunchberry, running club moss, and bracken ferns. Approximately one hundred feet to the north, at the bottom of a hill, is a small creek that meanders east towards the river. The river flows north to the Canadian border. This gives me a thought that puts a smile on my face: if ever I am forced to resort to the life of an outlaw, I have an easy escape route.

I was quite exhausted after carrying six loads of approximately eighty pounds each down to camp — it's amazing how many contrivances are required for an extended camping trip. The thick forest did not help my efforts. After everything is set up, I will dedicate time to clearing a trail from the Jeep to camp, and from camp to the river. I'm going to take a moment to record a brief inventory of my supplies.

For my lodgings I have a twelve-foot by nine-foot canvas outfitters tent with nylon floor, a nine-foot by nine-foot screen house, a three-man dome tent, a large canvas tarpaulin, a ten-foot by twenty-foot nylon tarp, and three eight-foot by eight-foot nylon tarps. I brought four sleeping bags, one fleece blanket, and two pillows for bedding. I also have a rope hammock and four camp chairs.

For kitchen supplies I have two fifty-quart coolers, a propane burner stove, a cooking pot and pan, basic utensils, a one-liter coffee thermos, a fillet knife, and a four-foot folding table.

My tools and hardware selection consists of a four-pound splitting axe, a carpenter saw, a drywall hammer, a spade shovel, a Leatherman multi-tool, nails, various sizes of nuts, bolts and washers, a multitude of rope, plywood and two-by-fours for a tent platform, and a basic tool kit with socket set and screw drivers. I keep a hunting knife with a six-inch blade attached to my belt. It should go without saying that I also have several rolls of duct tape.

I brought my laptop, which will only be used for writing my novel. For this journal, I am using a red notebook and #2 pencil. To charge the laptop I have a small solar-powered system: a sixty-watt panel, a twelve-volt gel cell battery, a twelve-volt deep-cycle battery, a voltage regulator, and a charge inverter. My only concern is the minimal amount of sunlight that penetrates the forest canopy; I may have to design a raised platform to get the panels above the shadows where they can reach more photons.

I brought twenty-five books, mostly naturalist guides, wilderness adventures and classic literature. I have fly fishing gear, including a small selection of tying materials. One of my goals this summer is to catch the elusive muskie on a fly rod. Here are many other items that I am not going to list, but which are necessary for this adventure.

After my efforts to haul this gear to camp, I wasn't interested in expending the energy to cut more firewood, so I am currently sitting outside on a folding chair beneath a dark and starry sky. With the exception of Sly, who is already asleep in the tent, I am completely alone. The nearest human is roughly two miles away, but that distance feels vast surrounded by this thick forest inhabited by a populace of wild animals. I will sleep in the three-man dome tent again tonight; tomorrow I build my tent platform and assemble my new home.

June 14 Tuesday

My first task today was to erect an awning to act as a rain shield over my tent. Before I could secure the awning, I had to build a ladder. I chopped down one of the aspen trees within camp that needed to be removed to make space for my tent, and cut it into pieces for a ladder, using twine to secure the steps.

I selected two aspen trees which were approximately

thirty feet apart and used the ladder to tie a section of half-inch rope between them about twelve feet up. This will act as a center truss to drape my canvas tarpaulin over. I stretched out the tarpaulin and attached eye-bolts to all four corners to act as grommets, and then pulled it up over the center truss and secured it with rope tied between the eye-bolts and proximal trees. The tarpaulin is roughly four-hundred square feet, but when I reduce the surface area from angle of pitch, I have approximately two-hundred and fifty square feet of coverage from rain and sun.

In an added effort to keep my tent clean and dry, I built a platform to get it up off the ground. I used six four-foot by eight-foot pieces of plywood with a frame built of two-by-fours. This gives me a foundation of twelve-feet by sixteen-feet, raised two-inches off the ground.

The sun shines bright above the trees and there is much bird song in the air. I'm going to scout out a suitable location beside the river to setup my hammock, and then spend the rest of daylight down there relaxing with a book and watching the slow moving water. I will speak with you tomorrow, dear journal friend of mine.

June 15 Wednesday

It's a bit funny to me, considering the vastness of this world, that wilderness is now a place to be traveled to, a destination for tourists, a location with specific borders, a setting distinguished from the cities that are now masters of the landscape.

It's only day three, or maybe four, yet already I feel at home while alone in this forest. Thinking about this causes a moment of guilt. Should I be missing my loved ones? What would Mayana think if I confessed that I was completely happy here, alone, without her?

Nonsense. I must focus on finishing camp, so that I can clear my thoughts and focus on the novel I am here to write. Today I will erect the canvas tent and dig the latrine pit. The sky is a bit grey, so I will work while I can before the rain.

I was able to dig the latrine pit before the rain began. I made it approximately four feet deep, and three foot by three foot wide. I then built a floor with spruce logs and leftover plywood. I cut a hole in the center of the plywood, and mounted a five-gallon pail with the bottom cut out. This will be my wilderness throne. It is approximately one-hundred yards from camp, and there are many mosquitoes. Tomorrow I will clear a trail to the throne and set up my canvas tent.

June 16 Thursday

I have lived in many bachelor pads during the thirteen years since I left the shelter of my parents' home and dove into this adult world completely unprepared. I have been subjected to gregarious influences, and I have surrendered to many temptations. I have been surrounded by a crowd of people, yet isolated in my own imagination. I have also experienced profound solitude. I have spent full days alone in a canoe, paddling the opposite direction of civilization, until my entire body ached, and then I paddled farther. Many nights were spent solo-camping deep in the mountains after spending the day hiking, only to pause and view a moose or bear, or follow the tracks of a mountain lion. I am at home in places so remote that there are no roads or towns on a 1:50,000 scale topo map. I am comfortable with loneliness of many forms. Yet here I am, alone in my own micro-wilderness, and I am experiencing doubt.

It has only been four or five days, but I think of the months to come here in the forest, the months that could be spent visiting family, or in the proximity of friends, or seeing coworkers five days a week, or any other number of social engagements, and I begin to feel lonesome. Lonesomeness is antithetical to my success, to my comfort, so I walk to the river, hoping to distract my thoughts. Along the way, I pause to view lichens growing on the bark of an aspen tree. I stop and study deer tracks in the soil. I stand beneath an old growth cedar and try to count the branches. I hear the birds chirping. A fish splashes from the surface of the river. I am not alone.

I spent the afternoon preparing a home of this forest. It is thoroughly enjoyable to me, breaking trail with only a machete and prune saw. I have decided to name the trail to the latrine "Newfound Glory." I had to make a slight detour from my original route to bypass the remains of a deer. It was a wolf kill, and the bones were scattered around with many teeth marks on them. I found the skull about one-hundred feet away on the other side of the creek. It must have been young, likely killed last autumn, judging by the size and condition of the skull. I took a moment to imagine its life. It would have been born late spring, after the forest had greened and fruits were plentiful. It learned to walk with wobbly legs shortly after birth, learned quickly to fear the howl of wolves, and adapted to the silence of the forest. Then the cold came, and its mother was lost, so it traveled the familiar trail along the creek shore, but this trail was also familiar to the wolves. The deer died in the forest where it was born, and next year, others will come in his place.

...

I've always considered myself quite handy. I enjoy building craft projects from scrap lumber, I find it entertaining to fix things, I can set camp by myself, and I can always start a fire in any weather with one match. Plus, I owned a small construction business at the age of twenty-three. All these skills were irrelevant to setting up a twelve-foot by nine-foot canvas outfitter tent. I may have been the first man these woods ever heard yell something as ridiculous as, "You fucking fuck of a fuckity fucker!"

I stretched out the canvas, stationed all the telescoping poles, and began to erect the frame. I got one wall up, then the next wall, and was working on a proud smile while I setup the center pole. I pulled it taut and it felt secure, so I stepped back, put my hands on waist, and watched everything collapse. I thought it was a fluke, and that my methods were good, so I attempted the same order of operations, and as the walls collapsed again, I tried to grab hold of the frame, which pulled me down into a pile of canvas and aluminum poles. This time, in a furious rage, I picked up the nearest tool — my shovel — and threw it into the forest like a javelin (it was truly an impressive pitch!), while simultaneously shouting, "Fuck you, you fucking fuckface!" I paced around in a fury until I encountered my splitting axe, which I proceeded to kick. This brought things into perspective. With a throbbing toe and a missing shovel, I re-investigated my strategy. This time it seemed easy, all I had to do was nail all four corners in place and then raise the center poles first. It worked, and by the time I stepped back to admire my new home, my toe no longer throbbed.

This is an impressive structure to see here in the middle of the woods. After making a bed of sleeping bags and fleece, I brought in the rest of my clothing and books.

Sly seems to enjoy his freedom here in the forest as much as I do. He runs off first thing in the morning, and I only see him several times a day when he stops in to check his food dish. We are both in the canvas tent tonight, and outside it is dark and wolves howl in the distance. Sly lies on the foot of my bed and perks up his ears every time they sing. I wonder if he may go wild and join their pack.

Mayana arrives tomorrow for her first visit and view of camp. She has decided to drive here on Friday nights and leave early Monday mornings in time for work. I wish you goodnight, dear journal friend, and tomorrow we will discuss another new adventure.

June 17 Friday

When I awoke this morning, my first thought was to heat up some oatmeal in the microwave, turn on the coffee pot, and then take a hot shower before checking my emails and the morning news. While still in semi-sleep and in the comfort of my sleeping bag, this seemed like a perfectly logical expectation. It was the sound of a woodpecker that changed my mind. I climbed out of bed and peeked out one of the screen windows. On an aspen tree only fifteen feet away was a male pileated woodpecker. He was low on the tree, about ten feet up, and I watched him work at chiseling the circumference. What a life that must be.

I emerged from the tent and felt the sun on my face. The air was cool, and there was a mist that dangled from the tops of the trees. Sly bolted into the forest, and I walked to the river. There were several otters treading water midstream, until they saw me and went under. I sat on a log and watched the dragonflies chasing morning mosquitoes. This is a complex world that no words can explain.

Mayana arrived mid-afternoon with her dog Canyon. I was at camp staring at the ashes of last night's fire. It is easy to get lost in thought while here alone. I take this as a sign that, when it comes time, I will be able to fully focus on my novel. I haven't started yet, but that is because I haven't yet had a chance to set up the solar panels that will be required to power my laptop. While I write this journal with pencil and notebook, my novel will require the abilities of a computer, which requires electricity. I will spend my time with Mayana this weekend, and then get focused on writing the novel next week. There is plenty of time here in the woods. It's amazing how much time can exist in the absence of a clock.

When Mayana arrived, she carried a crate full of milk cartons that were filled with ice, and a duffle bag packed full of Clif bars, brats, instant coffee, and vodka. She is the most beautiful woman I have ever seen. We filled the cooler and then dove into the tent. Sometime shortly before dark, we reemerged and started a fire.

Mayana sat on the ground beside me in my camp chair. The fire roared orange and yellow and blue, and we watched the sparks flicker up like fireflies. The small clearing above us revealed a sky perforated with starlight. This indeed is a mysterious world. I have read a fair number of books, studied science, and listened objectively to the arguments for religion, but nothing, absolutely nothing, explains the thoughts that transpire while in the stillness of a nocturnal forest.

June 18 Saturday

The rain was heavy when it came late last night. We drank a couple bottles of wine by lantern light while wrapped tightly in the sleeping bags, and then slept solidly until morning. Raindrops on the roof of a tent are the greatest sedative I know. When I awoke and climbed from the tent, I saw the rain barrels full of fresh rainwater. This was a glorious sight, because now my limited supply of drinking water wouldn't have to be used for boiling coffee or washing dishes.

The clouds were still low and grey as we sat beside the fire and Mayana cooked bacon. The dampness of a forest has a smell completely unique, and the air between the trees seems as green as the leaves and needles. Beneath the retreating storm is a faint pink where the sun burns on the horizon. I saw a painting once that did this justice, but even here in real life, the image is beyond the grasp of definition and exists like a fantasy, always just past the reach of my fingers. At least on canvas, the illusion could be touched.

After breakfast, we took a walk through the woods. The forest is a moody maiden, and she is most temperamental after a storm. It is after a storm that mosquitoes rage in dense and violent swarms. This is when the spiders work vigorously to rebuild their webs the rain and wind destroyed. The ferns, which have grown above my waist, are wet and seem to reach out for me as I pass, drenching my pants and shirt and boots. The hills are slick and the ground is soft. But the wood ticks love it. They seem to thrive in these conditions, and no matter if I tuck my pants into my boots or my shirt into my pants, or if my head is covered in netting, they still find their way to my flesh.

I have a hate–love relationship with the wood ticks. I hate them for their plans to suckle my blood, for the diseases they carry, and for their general repugnance. But I love them because they act as a regulator. They are part of the reason this region of the world remains largely uninhabited by mankind, and I have heard many hardy outdoorsmen and women say they stay entirely out of the forest during tick season. The mosquitoes also help reduce the population, but everyone knows of the mosquito, and they have received the bulk of credit and publicity. Fewer know of the mosquito's silent, and perhaps more despicable, accomplice. But if it weren't for the wood tick, these forests would be comfortable, and so this river, which is scenic and pristine, would be lined with mansions and tennis courts. I've seen it happen before, in lands not blessed by the presence of wood ticks.

So, as much as I hate peeling their brainless bodies from my flesh, as disgusted as I am by seeing hordes of them scampering up my legs, as much time as they add to my nightly chores (since I must pick them from Sly and myself), I can say, with tongue under foot, that I am glad they exist here. But still, after returning from a walk with Mayana in our woods and watching a horde of them scamper up her legs, I am upset by their existence. It is a hate–love relationship we share, and today, hate is winning.

June 19 Sunday

It is a fact that in all of art, the most soothing and serene images always portray water — whether clouds, river, ocean or rain. The reason seems obvious, but also multi-dimensional. You could draw the conclusion that we are comforted by sights of the water from which our primordial ancestors emerged, or that we feel safe knowing water — the substance of life — is within reach. These are both true, but I believe there is another truth. Water is a tranquilizer, it has a sedative effect that creates a sense of calmness, and every organic creature is influenced by its power. Like Narcissus beside the pond, gazing into his eternal beauty, water holds the reflection of our instinctual desires.

This was the topic of conversation as we portaged the canoe from the trailer through the thick woods to the river. The mosquitoes are assailants of opportunity, and they didn't deny themselves the opportunity to take advantage of two humans whose hands were occupied with carrying a canoe and were left defenseless. Their screams buzzing in my ears were more painful than their bite. We walked fast, trying not to trip over objects hidden on the forest floor, but I still felt to be pricked by a thousand needles.

When we reached the river, we wasted no time loading and shoving off. Around midstream, the breeze gained enough velocity to blow away most of the mosquitoes. The current was slow, making the surface appear calm as a lake, and so it was easy to paddle upstream.

About fifty rods upstream we encountered a mild riffle where the water got shallower, and boulders came close to the surface. We meandered through the obstacles and continued around a sharp bend. The river opened up into a deep and wide clearing. Here we saw an osprey perched in a tree beside its nest. While the osprey, like many other birds of prey, have adapted to areas dense with human population, when I see them in a wild setting, they are more majestic, and appear as natural as the trees. Here their habits and motives are the same as a thousand years ago. I think about how much the manmade world has changed in a thousand years, and I envy these birds. Do they know? Are they in communication with their domesticated brethren who live in concrete jungles? Are these birds who live here the reclusive sort who migrate to the wild by choice? Do they silently mock their civilized brethren who live in cities and battle airplanes, pollution, and noise, just for the chance of easily obtained carrion?

This animal perched beside the river is free. He has always been free. Makes me wonder if freedom is as valuable if you have never experienced its opposite. I am familiar with the restrictions of contemporary society, and so I envy his ignorance.

While I am aware that my freedom here is ephemeral, for inevitably I must return to the world of men, I feel more connected to this place than any home where I have ever lived. It's more than the silence. It's more than the view. It's more than the animals. There is a subliminal force that fills my veins when I walk alone through the forest. There exists an inaudible song only heard by those who are at peace below the canopy of leaves, beside a gentle stream, and are comfortable with the confrontation of darkness.

June 20 Monday

I have always been an outsider, and I blame this on my thoughts. I have never been able to follow the methods of another without first testing them for myself, and the very notion of authority figures fills me with an insatiable urge to rebel. Perhaps this is a condition natural to most of mankind, but I can only speak for myself. I have always been an outsider, and I *credit* this to my thoughts. The source is creativity, for I always feel the desire to recreate something and make it my own, whether that be a principle, a purpose, or an object. It is never as good if it belongs to somebody else. If it was not designed by my own mind then how can I trust it? This has given me a disability in society, as if I carry a disease that repels others from my sense of independence. They find me awkward, and view me as though an alien figure.

If creativity is a disease, then people are the cure. If we're all born with this disease and are slowly but steadily cured of it as we grow into knowing more and more people — their experiences and expectations and ideas and lessons — and thus become influenced by their very existence, then eventually the disease of creativity is expelled from our mind and replaced by information. Information is the destroyer of creativity because it fills the mind with answers about how things are, and with every new piece of information, there is one less wonder in the world to solve with creative imagination. Through the world of media and social interactions, we are constantly gathering information, and slowly the mind is relieved of the disease of creativity.

One day we may decide that the inherent disease was better than this palliative health, and try to recover it. But there's no simple intravenous injection for creativity — at least not yet. So how do you get it back? Do you surround yourself with creative people — if a creative person can actually coexist within a group — and hope that their disease is contagious? It is not. The only way you can catch it is by being born, seeing everything new and fresh and imagining why it is what it is, and using this power of thought to create your own solipsistic masterpiece. The irony is that this very solipsism of your mind can drive you insane, and this is the disease. However, it's a disease that can only be diagnosed by those whom have already been cured. They will view creativity as a synonym for insanity, but sanity is relevant to the information they have acquired by comparing themselves to other people. So let me repeat the original hypotheses as a statement of theory: Creativity is a disease common to the human mind which can only be cured by the conscious decision to develop an affinity for the information acquired through the coercion of other people.

The beautiful part is that you can decide to reject their cure. You can decide to live with the disease and experience a life of confusion and social awkwardness. Confusion is the greatest gift because it analyzes the data you've been given and decides this is not enough, that there is a void, and this realization inspires the mind to design its own answers.

These were the thoughts I considered as I walked

through the dark and damp morning forest after guiding Mayana to her car so she could drive to work. As we walked to the car, we heard a bear shuffling through the trees. It was loud and slow and made a grunting, mooing sound similar to a Black Angus bull. We paused in a grove of beaked hazelnuts and listened to it pass through the thick trees approximately fifty feet to our west. After Mayana got in her car to drive back to town, I returned to the forest and knelt down to pause and think.

I imagined myself living like the bear, born in the forest without any foreign influence, and living mostly alone to design my own habits, abilities, and ideas of the world. The world would be whatever I created, and there would be no contradicting information to tell me I was wrong. I stood up and walked back to camp, and I felt confused. I was disoriented by the idea that men should ever leave the forest. Here there is solitude and I find myself in long moments of wonder. To wonder is truly wonderful, and I enjoy contemplating thoughts that never occurred to me while living inside the walls of a city, confined by the limiting walls of society. Here I am free, and that is the only way I can be me.

There is much work to do around camp, and I should set up my solar power system so that I can begin the novel. Instead I will spend the rest of morning sitting on the log beside the river.

June 21 Tuesday

This morning I drew up a schematic for a camp shower, but before assembling it, I decided to sit by the river and watch the water for a while. I was watching a beaver retrieve branches from the far shore and carry them midstream to consume. I watched the beaver, but my thoughts wandered off to memories of my past. I thought I had discovered some grandiose notion about life while sitting silently in seclusion, so I returned to camp with intentions to write it. After I sharpened my pencil and opened this notebook, I realized the notion was inexpressible. I sat here for many moments trying to define it. I spoke to myself as if a separate person, as if I were both teacher and pupil. It occurred to me that no words by the tongue of man can express the simplicities of a quiet land, so I returned to the river.

The sun burned hot, and the air was humid, so I took a cleansing swim in the river. The water felt cool, and as I treaded water in the mild velocity of midstream, I imagined a giant muskie passing under and discovering my bare feet and thinking they'd make a delicious treat. I returned to shore and began using my t-shirt to dry with. My legs and abdomen were covered with leeches. This inspired me to setup my shower, so I returned to camp. I entered the tent to change into dry clothes and saw a copy of *Desert Solitaire* lying on the pillow. I will build the shower tomorrow.

June 22 Wednesday

People always surprise me. I may be antisocial and perhaps a touch misanthropic, but that's only because I care so damn much about people. This is a bit of a paradox, I admit, but it's my love for people that makes me distant. It's in our nature to take advantage of those who show concern and compassion for us. This is a theory that has been proven true many times in my life. I have offered my heart and my favors to many only to be taken advantage of, and, in honesty, I have done the same. If I were given a podium with an audience of all the world, my only question would be, "Are you all just like me?" I think the answer is yes. I think we all experience the same denial, that we all reach out and offer everything at some point in life, and once we are denied, we learn to defend ourselves from ever making that same mistake. We develop an impenetrable shell and begin to blame others for our pain. But we are just like them. I have explored the wilderness in many formats, and all I have searched for is a reason why people make me so uncomfortable. I don't have any answers, but the trees give me peace.

It is dark. I don't know the time, for I don't wear a watch, but the moon is near the middle of the sky. The mosquitoes are mostly gone now and the air is quiet around me. In the stillness of midnight, my thoughts find the room to roam and explore new potential. There is a chill in the night, so I pull myself closer to the fire. It is dark and an owl makes its presence known. The voices in my head fade and are muted by the silence of a nocturnal forest. It is this silence that fills me with gratitude. There is discomfort, for I am alone and this is always uneasy, but I am happy because I am free, and I know that when the sun rises tomorrow, I can design a new day however I please.

June 23 Thursday

It is early morning but the sun hasn't risen and I have yet to sleep. It is dark outside and I lie awake in the tent. My eyes are heavy, and I feel ready for dreams, but there are sounds surrounding me in the forest.

It's amazing how disturbing the claws of mice can seem while alone in a dark wood. I have faced death in the form of wild creatures many times: encountering two grizzlies while alone in a deep canyon in some isolated Wyoming mountains; stepping over a rattlesnake that could easily rise up and bite me between the legs; walking through a wintry wood on the fresh trail of a mountain lion who was likely perched in a tree waiting silently for the next mammal to make dinner out of; being within one hundred feet of a pack of howling wolves in a dark wilderness; or being chased out of a trout stream by a herd of wild, stampeding buffalo. There have been many encounters when I could have perished as a result of wild forces. Despite my survival of all these experiences, the mysterious sound of mice clawing up my tent and rustling around on the forest floor nearby is enough to make me grip my knife handle firmly under the pillow and keep the headlamp strapped around my head.

I know they are small, weighing a couple ounces, without claws or fangs, and that their greatest threat lies hidden in their scat, but still, the imagination expounds their sounds to that of giant beasts, and the darkness makes every beast seem a threat. So I turn on my lantern, pour a mourning drink, and scribble my thoughts in this pad. Imagine if I were attacked by a thousand mice; that death wouldn't be so bad, for I would die in my home. It would be a happy death to die in the wild. So I turn off the lantern, place my knife under the pillow, remove my headlamp, and place it beside the bed. Now I will walk out, into the darkness, and the sounds of nocturnal beasts will not threaten me.

June 24 Friday

Today is beautiful and I am in love with a river. It's not necessarily the water I love, though the intermingling of cool dampness with my skin is refreshing and definitely invigorates my mind. It is not only the calming reflectivity of its placid surface, though from an aesthetic perspective, the mirrored mosaic is often more captivating than the surrounding landscape, and I am awed by the way these colors all swirl together, as if an oil paint has been touched to a canvas by a master painter. It may not even be the substrate, the way my senses are heightened when my bare feet transition from muck to sand to gravel and back again. I couldn't even narrow it down to the blooming lily pads and the dragonflies that hover there, even though I am often drawn to long moments of speculation by their aerobatics. Certainly the fish are great, and the pursuit of them keeps me testing myself with new methods, but even on days without a catch, I am satisfied. I consider all of these attributes, as well as the way the sun feels on my ears as I make a cast, and I know that I am in love with a mystery.

I returned to camp after spending the early hours of today in the river with my fly rod. I was making long casts with a large fly hoping for a muskie, but there were no takers. They call muskies the fish of ten-thousand casts, and I am learning why. By the time I peel out sixty to seventy feet of line, make the cast, let my fly settle below the surface, and then retrieve it, I have spent approximately fifty seconds. If I use this figure as an average, then I could potentially make seventy-five casts per hour. Reduce that by 25 percent for time spent between casts to consider my next move, and then make the cast, and I'm looking at roughly fifty-six per hour. So that's over one-hundred and seventy hours of casting. After the three hours today, there is a lot of time left to go. This thought gives me a sense of thrill.

I read a book once titled *There's More to Fishing than Catching Fish*, and I believe that to be true. Unless you are fishing for sustenance, in which case catching a fish is the only thing that matters, and the thoughts and feelings that occur during are only distractions. I have always believed that if you are fishing for a meal, then live bait is your best option, but if you are fishing for pleasure, then fly rod and hand-tied fly are the preferred method. I have tried to express this sentiment to friends of mine who pursue fishing as a competitive sport, and who only know it as an attempt to capture, or rather, defeat nature. I have always failed because sentiments can only be learned by the individual, never taught secondhand. You cannot explain the true grace of fly fishing, how it feels to be completely immersed in something simple and splendid, yet absolutely complex and arcane. No, you cannot express it to a person who has never experienced it, a person who doesn't have it in the very source-blood of their memories, for it is there that we exist while alone in a silent and salient river, someplace deep in the past while we cast forward. But you cannot convince a person to understand this who has never experienced the sound of water flowing around them, or the texture of slippery stones beneath slick waders, or the tug of a large trout on a fine tippet and the sight of rapids downstream, any more than you can get a fish to walk on dry land, or the river to turn and flow up hill. Or, as I'm learning, a muskie to bite on the first cast.

June 25 Saturday

Mayana and I sat beside a fire on this fine evening. Wine has a tendency to persuade my thoughts toward the sentimental. After the second bottle was dry, I tried to express these thoughts to her in a somber monologue. She sat on the ground beside me and listened without interruption.

I won't try to recount what I said word for word, because it is late now, and she is asleep while I make this entry in the tent by dim headlamp. While the thoughts are fresh in my mind, I will try to repeat them.

We had gotten on the topic of our lives together, and how it had been difficult to live frugally and save up enough money to make this adventure real, but now that it is real, it seems like it has always been this way. I started thinking about my past, and the wine may have influenced my perception, because I said something like, *Have I imagined it all? That seems to be the only explanation that explains anything anymore. How else could all of this exist? How else could I be so happy and yet filled with so much pain? How else can any of this make any damn sense? It certainly doesn't make any damn sense, but somehow that is okay, and I make peace with knowing nothing, and that only makes sense if I am living something imagined rather than real. Real must be empirical and so proven and reproducible, but I have never experienced anything so acute and so dull as being real, so I am living in my imagination and that means I imagined you. Maybe I'm not so bad after all, if I could create somebody like you. Perhaps I should stop wondering and complaining and enjoy this mystery for being indescribable. So I'd like to watch you dance for a while. I hope you enjoy the attention.*

She replied, *I will dance for you, but only because you have eyes like the forest.*

I didn't really know what she meant, but this didn't matter because it made sense in the moment. We were out of wine, but the night was full and we weren't going to waste that.

June 26 Sunday

I truly enjoy cutting firewood. I enjoy carrying the saw in my hand as I search for a fallen tree that has dried to the perfect burning point. I enjoy the sound of the saw and the smell of the wood being sliced. I enjoy the ants and spiders that climb off the bark and up the hand that holds the tree in place. I enjoy the pain in my muscles as I decide to cut one more. I enjoy the sticky sap on my fingers and the small piles of sawdust on the forest floor. I enjoy the scrapes on my arms after I carry a full load back to camp. I enjoy dividing the wood into three piles based on size and dryness. I enjoy selecting the perfect piece to be used as a poking stick and keeping it beside me until everything else has burned and I toss it in the fire. I enjoy thinking I have cut more wood than I will need, only to be proven wrong by midnight with plenty of energy to stay awake and burn more. I enjoy stumbling through darkness in search of another load, and wandering deep into the woods until I can only see the faint flickering flame. I enjoy the sound of a cracking branch as it echoes through the night. I enjoy staying awake until the beer is gone and then extinguishing the fire with my urine. I enjoy the final look through the screen window of my tent at the smoldering embers, knowing they will still be warm in the morning. I enjoy the smoky smell on my pillow when I awake the next day. I enjoy the simplicity of it all, and knowing not a single light switch or electrical outlet was required.

June 27 Monday

I am a scientist. At least that's what every personality test I have taken since junior high tells me. The paradox is that I often despise the sciences. It is the mission of science to tell us why things are what they are, which is certainly a noble pursuit. However, this greatly inhibits the freedom of imagination. If you only gather your beliefs from a textbook or classroom and use these cookie cutter ideas to analyze the world around you, then you will only ever know the world the way others have known it before you. So I often enjoy sitting for long moments of speculation, looking at something as though my eyes were the first to ever view it, and in so doing, I am eliminating the knowledge gathered and passed down from generations, and I am wondering. The irony is that these wondering thoughts are often inexplicable, as they exist internal. But what I know is my own, and I have earned my ideas through the application of our species' greatest tool — the imagination.

It is easy to get lost in wandering thoughts while alone in the forest, which strengthens my opinion that this is how we were designed to be, and that living the busy life of a city only congests our thoughts and distracts us from the greatest application of our mind — to let it roam freely. I have discovered a paradox of sorts that I will try to explain. While living in a city and working full time, there was this idea of the "Real World," and that was something tangible, and a place where others lived with me. While I was there, the imagination was intangible, and when there was time, I lived in it alone. Here in the forest, what I used to consider the "Real World" is reserved for the imagination and remains intangible, while the imagination is omnipresent and I can reach out and touch it.

What I'm saying is this: the life I currently live is the one I always imagined, and now that I'm in it, my imagination has merged with the "Real World." Now that I'm living in my imagined life, the "Real World" where I used to live seems imaginary.

June 28 Tuesday

It has been two weeks, and I've already fully diminished my first #2 pencil. It is also my only #2 pencil. I will have to make a walk to the road so I can call Mayana and alert her to this situation. I am writing with a nub no longer than the tip of my index finger, and I thought my handwriting was sloppy with a proper utensil. The mosquitoes don't help anything, but I'm not sure they ever have. Tonight they are especially disruptive, and even though I sit two feet from a smoky fire, they are undeterred and have acquired their target — my entire body. The squiggly lines scraping across this page from dragging my pencil as I slap one from my skin looks like the jottings of a madman, and that is precisely what these flying buzzing beasts have created. For the first thirty minutes, I tolerated them with a sense of comical pride, and imagined that by allowing them to feast from my flesh, I would develop skin like a buffalo hide and become impenetrable to their forces. If this is possible, it certainly takes longer than thirty minutes to cultivate that sort of adaptation. I will surrender myself to the tent and hope there are no wood ticks there to join me.

I am alone but not lonely — not in the way I used to get while living in bachelor pads and finding myself with no company on a Friday night. But this tent does feel hollow, even though Sly sleeps at my feet. My dying headlamp only slightly illuminates the space around me in yellows and greys. It is dark outside these canvas walls and the silence echoes with unseen marauders. This heightens my audio receptors, and I find myself perplexed and thrilled by every crackle of a leaf on the forest floor. I imagine myself being the last man alive on Earth. I would like to explore this idea further, but it will have to remain internal tonight, for this is the end of my pencil lead.

July 1 Friday

The best part of being entirely alone is the opportunity to engage in conversations with myself. I used to get so busy living in the city and its perpetual social interactions that the man in the mirror was a stranger. There was not time to communicate clearly with my *self*. When I was in the presence of others — whether people in my company or unknowns across a crowded room — my attention was focused on them and the amazing differences between each one. I lost myself in the studious occupation of trying to understand others, and trying to make them understand me. Through retrospective eyes, I now see that understanding was never achieved. Perhaps an alternate and more socially acceptable form of understanding was achieved — *mis*understanding. That was the only way we ever knew each other: strangers in company occupying proximal spaces but never having the time to recognize the internal mechanizations of the person whose shadow follows us everywhere. I always felt that distance, but while being submersed in it there was no way to identify what it was that I specifically felt. Here in the forest with the trees and sky and hidden animal eyes as my only witness, I have discovered a new understanding of my *self*.

If there were anyone here to hear me, and I were so bold as to try and summarize what I have learned during my two weeks of solitude, I would say, "Be silent until you can communicate clearly with yourself." But that wouldn't do, because those would be my words, not theirs. I would insist that they entirely ignore anything I have to say, and that they answer their own questions. Whatever I have to offer is only mine and if we are to become truly independent individuals — the way we are designed to be — then they shouldn't even ask for my opinion because it would only interfere with their own.

Currently, I sit beside a small fire while Mayana sleeps in the tent. A light rain is falling, and I enjoy the way it sounds when each drop makes contact with the open pages of this notebook. She arrived late this evening with my new supplies, including a dozen #2 pencils. She made a strange face when she noticed my elation after seeing these new pencils, and I now understand that face to have been one of disappointment that I was more excited about my pencils than about seeing her. It's been three days since my previous entry and there have been so many thoughts building up that I was filled with anticipation of their release. The moment I sat down to write them, they became blurry and fleeting. I started a fire and mostly ignored Mayana, so she went into the tent earlier than usual. It's getting difficult to write in the rain, and I am concerned about ruining these pages, so I will now go join her. I have missed her and am curious to hear how her life has been this previous week.

July 2 Saturday

This morning Mayana and I slept in late and would have slept later if not for the dogs. They both became alert and made anxious noises while running their paws inside the doorway of the tent. I crawled out of bed and tried to calm them, and then I peeked out all the windows. I could see nothing and presumed whatever had caused them to get excited was either hidden from my view, or had dispersed. I released them and they bolted into the forest heading south. I yelled for them to return, but they were oblivious of me. After thirty minutes of calling out their names and whistling, I decided it was time to find them, so I grabbed my machete and asked Mayana to remain at camp in case they returned.

I was deep into the forest with neither sight nor sound of the dogs. I heard thunder and looked up at low dark clouds churning in the sky. A wind came on strong and the rain fell hard at slants through the trees. I continued to go further into the forest.

When I found the dogs, they were circling a spruce tree, looking towards the top while barking and clawing. I approached and could see nothing, so I grabbed the dogs by their collars and began guiding them towards camp. I was soaking wet and the sky was turning green. A gust of wind rushed through the trees, I heard branches cracking, and then a thud and subsequent squeal directly behind me. I turned around and saw an opossum that had fallen from the spruce. I was able to hold Sly, but Canyon ripped through his collar and pursued the opossum. The varmint was quick to return to the tree, and I had to secure my belt around Canyon's neck to force him back to camp.

When the three of us returned to camp soaking wet, we found Mayana in the screen house brewing coffee over the propane stove. The wind was strong, and the flames from the stove rose violently in blue and yellow. Mayana looked unconcerned, so I dried off the dogs and myself as best as possible with the one towel we keep at camp, and then Mayana joined us in the tent with fresh instant coffee. We spent the rest of the day reading while listening to the storm and wondering which tree would fall on us first.

By the time Mayana prepared for bed and I sat down to make this entry, I had gotten well into the novel *Narcissus and Goldmund*, by Hermann Hesse. My favorite line so far has been, "Insofar as I have come to know people, we all have a slight tendency, especially while we are young, to confuse our wishes with predestination." I sat for a long moment wondering if I am guilty of confusing my wish of becoming a novelist with an inherent sense of predestination. For as long as I can remember, I have had it in my mind that I would become a writer of great books. I often sit and ruminate on the idea of being an accomplished writer. It feels so real in my imagination that I can almost convince myself it has already been accomplished. I know it will not come easily, and I have yet to begin the novel I came here to write. My thoughts have been on it much, and I am beginning to see the protagonist and his journey more clearly. When it is vivid, and when I know not only the how but also the why of the story, then I will begin. I've written some lines and a few passages as they enter my thoughts, but have yet to establish any time-sequence of events.

It is my intention to emulate what I enjoy most about books. Books by their nature are difficult to define, because they exist subjectively in the mind of the reader, and the author may have had an entirely different intention. For me, books offer the ability to see into another person's existence, to view the world through their eyes, to share their experiences as a participant, so that I can gain empathy for the reasoning of humans completely different than me. If a book is good, and most of them are in some fashion, then at the end I feel to be in unison with the characters, and their experiences were my own and I will remember them for the power I felt.

I don't want to write for fame or fortune — if those were my desires, I would go into music or acting. I want to write because of the books I have enjoyed and because of all the books I will never read, those multitudinous titles I can only imagine the contents of but will never know from cover to cover. If I could choose fame or fortune, it would be fortune, because I could retire to a quiet place in the woods and spend my days reading. On my deathbed, the only thing I will regret is all the books I never read.

July 3 Sunday

I often feel in close contact with the past, and I want to relive that glory and adventure. The past feels so proximal in my memory until my feet try to step into it, and like a river that has gone dry, I am left barren and thirsty for what is lost.

This morning I was sitting on the muddy shore of the creek and thinking about the job I gave up to pursue the grandiose notion of writing in the forest. What I may have failed to mention earlier was that when I met with my supervisor to give my notice of resignation, he attempted to persuade me to stay by offering an assignment coveted by all adventure-seeking scientists. Every year, one member of our crew was selected to spend six weeks studying glacial streams in Antarctica. The dates were mid-November through end of December, which is the summer season in the southern hemisphere, meaning the daytime temps would rise into the forties, and the selected person would spend their time there sleeping in snow caves, flying in helicopters, snowshoeing across the most remote landscapes on Earth, and being completely responsible for monitoring stream gaging stations. He provided a persuasive argument, but my mind had been made. What value would my current adventure hold without the sacrifice?

I have always been a writer, but to dedicate myself completely to this task I needed to dive fully in. Perhaps I could have postponed this adventure one more year, spent those six weeks in Antarctica, but time is flimsy and circumstance greatly capricious, so there would have been no guarantees I would have made it here the following year. I think about how great six weeks in Antarctica could have been, and I am glad to be here instead. I have had many adventures, and writing will be one of them. I want to stay true to my craft and honor creativity above all. My position as a Hydrographer for the U.S. Geological Survey was the greatest job a man of my predilection could have. My days were spent wading across mountainous trout streams or hiking into high plains rivers to collect water samples and record discharge measurements. It was the best kind of adventure — the kind that was funded by an employer who paid me to participate. Dedication to science was the founding principle, and desire for adventure was the leading requirement. During winter I would get dropped out from helicopters in places so remote only the animals ever saw them, and from there I would snowshoe miles to a frozen river and use an ice bar to open a section then slice my way in. I enjoyed the pristinity of winter landscapes as much as I enjoyed the fact that one mistake could result in a frozen death.

In the summer, I would drive long distances down bumpy two-track roads that fewer than ten vehicles a year traveled, and then hike the remaining miles along the fresh tracks of mountain lions, around large piles of grizzly bear scat, beside bull moose, and find my way to a trout stream. After my job duties were performed, it was time to assemble the fly rod and spend my lunch break casting for trout. These fish were so prolific at high altitudes where humans rarely visited that I often tried not to catch a fish, just so it would feel like more of an accomplishment when I did. I was inspired by the mountains, and my overall way of life was influenced by their danger and simplicity. In certain circles I was known as the *Last Mountain Man*, and though I knew men more deserving of this title than myself, I still enjoyed it.

I miss the mountains of Wyoming, not for what they were, but for what they made me. It's better to have that memory than to not, but it is difficult to live with experiences that will never be experienced again.

I have been known by many nicknames in my life, some of them I approved, while others were meant to ridicule. Of those I approved, my most cherished was *Riverfeet*. It took many mountainous trout streams and raging torrents to earn this title. Many slick cobble stones and partially frozen surfaces. Many collected water samples and many lost trout. Many angry moose and many stampeding buffalo. Many frozen waders and many wet socks. Many summer suns and many treacherous storms. Many tangled lines and many moments of respite.

I sit at camp and try to focus on the future rather than the past. When I return to society after this adventure and begin a new career and new life, new people will know me, and I will become a new person. They will not know who I was in the forest, and there will be no time or opportunity to show them. When I change, the person I was will be forgotten. It will be as if the life I lived with all those unique and powerful experiences has been erased and become inconsequential to the new people in my life. But those memories will live inside me. If I am strong, those actions will survive and guide me through the new passages. If I am kind, I will focus on learning about theirs.

July 4 Monday

Independence Day. I hadn't even thought about that until Mayana mentioned she would be watching fireworks tonight over Lake Bemidji with a friend from work. Independence Day, and I will be alone. Independence Day, and I will be free. Independence Day, and I am as independent as ever I could hope to be.

Independence Day has generally been for me an opportunity to congregate with friends amongst large crowds, usually in proximity of a lake or river or sea, and drink copious amounts of alcohol and cheer at the fire-lit sky with inebriated shouts and masculine laughter. It was typically an excuse to be rowdy and obnoxious, and to celebrate our freedom with arrogance and danger. I remember a year in my early twenties, loading up a caravan of four cars with young men seeking adventure, and traveling to a festival called Taste of Minnesota, which was held annually in St. Paul. The event was full of live music, greasy food, carnival games, souvenirs, booze, and young women scantily dressed. It was a busy crowd packed shoulder to shoulder in the humid air, and it was filled with gluttony, sweat, and beer. What better way to represent being free? Or so I used to think.

Imagine, if you will, more than twenty young men carrying plastic cups loaded with beer, and moving as one single unit through a dense crowd. Surely you have seen us, or others of our kind, and most likely you tried to avoid eye contact, and whispered after we passed about what a disgrace the young hoodlums of today had become. If this is true, then you were correct — we were a disgrace; and it was most exciting. Flinging our cigarette butts into a crowd, tossing our empty cups onto the ground, tipping over dumpsters, threatening any group of young men who passed, and whistling at any female above the age of sixteen wearing short shorts, or any shorts at all. We were fueled by competition with each other, and we were empowered by beer and the belief of eternity. We were immortals above the law, and no consequence could threaten us. I often wonder what happened to those few I spent my youth in battle beside, those select individuals I was drawn to simply by coincidence, whom I joined forces with against an unknown future and a world so large that we depended upon each other because none of us knew a damn thing, and we were all so wise.

I left that life after many bloody knuckles and many knives in the back. We could only survive so long as one, and eventually disbanded into private sects. I moved away into the Northwoods to regroup and make sense of a past and pursue a new future. I found a new constitution for living while I was alone in the forest for the first time, and I rediscovered the simple pleasures that had been passed down to me by my father, uncle, and grandfather. This mostly involved fishing and camping, but it also included retrospective thought and deep ruminations while silent and surrounded by natural landscapes. My wandering thoughts often guided me through the maze of my past.

I cannot forget those adventures, some criminal, others just foolish. Alone here in the forest, I can feel the presence of those young men I once considered so powerful and important. I will forever wonder what happened to them, and though many of us separated as enemies, I remember them only as the friends who forged my life and instilled in me whatever strengths I have earned through the trials of youth in America. I can only hope they have found a semblance of the peace and independence I have, and on this Day of Independence, I hope they think of me while watching a fire-lit sky, and I hope there is someone special beside them to share this event with.

I am alone, and I am happy. I share this natural kingdom with a diverse sect of wild individuals who, since the days of their ancestors, have always been independent and self-sustaining. This is a mysterious world I have found in the forest, it is haunted not by ghosts and goblins, but by specters of my own memory and experience. I sit alone beside the fire with a sports bottle half-full of vodka and Tang, and I imagine the parties happening across this country in cities and towns, and I do not miss it. I have had my fill of their social debaucheries, and I have decided instead to live as the animals live — except I live with a memory foreign from any this forest could know.

July 5 Tuesday

I slept late this morning and awoke beside an empty bottle of vodka and a copy of *Babbitt*, by Sinclair Lewis. The book was opened to a page where I had marked a passage that struck me as relevant to my current condition. I read it again: "For many minutes, for many hours, for a bleak eternity, he lay awake, shivering, reduced to primitive terror, comprehending that he had won freedom, and wondering what he could do with anything so unknown and so embarrassing as freedom."

I felt free and confused, and these words seemed to have been written about me, so I jumped from bed as if I were transported into a fictional novel. I thought about the year of frugality and the sacrifices that brought me here, and I knew that this was surreal. I wanted to retain this sense of fiction and let it guide my imagination, so I stumbled down to the river and dove in fully clothed. It was cool and enlivening, and I dug my toes into the mucky bottom. I waded out to midstream, as far as my feet could touch, and swam out to where the current reached its maximum velocity. I lay on my back and drifted downstream while watching the clouds above me. I landed on a large boulder at the upstream side of a riffle where I sat and watched the small fish suckle the skin from my toes and legs. I watched the surrounding landscape with great curiosity, and I wanted to discover the words that could describe it in all its unspoiled beauty. I have been lucky enough to find myself alone many times in scenic landscapes, and someday I will synthesize the proper combination of words that can express each unique view for its majestic splendor.

I found myself thinking back to a trip I took alone into the Wind River Mountains of Wyoming. It was late spring so the river was high and raging through the steep canyon. I hiked up the mountain along a path mostly used by elk and the predators who pursued them. I climbed up to the top where the river rushed over a great fall, and then boulder-hopped out to the edge where I let my legs dangle over. I could see far into the basin, out through the great distances where I had recently traveled by automobile, and all of those machines that made up my daily routine seemed alien, as if I had imagined them and the only truth was this river and the mountain and the animal tracks that cut through the trees.

It had gotten dark early that night as a storm came in. I lay in my tent and it flapped and filled with air like a parachute. The sky flickered with bright bolts of electricity, and the thunder was so close I felt its vibration in my chest. I thought I would die alone in the mountains, and it would be days, perhaps weeks, before anyone found me. I thought that was okay. I had lived a good life, and since death was coming for me anyway, this would be a happy way to go. I unzipped my tent and a gust of wind and rain rushed in. I stepped out and saw the green sky above me. I was entirely alone and it would be more dangerous to scale down the muddy mountain than to stay at camp. The tent protected me from nothing except getting wet, so I decided to be done with it and I found a tall pine tree that I leaned upon and watched the storm. It was violent and powerful, and I remember thinking how weak I was at the mercy of nature.

When I woke up the next day, the sky was pink and the surrounding land glistened in the morning sun. Raindrops dripped from all the foliage, and my entire body was soaked. I packed up my wet tent and headed down the mountain in soppy boots. Two-hundred yards downhill I crossed the tracks of a grizzly bear fresh in the morning mud. I paused on one knee and surveyed the landscape. The river was loud beside me and I wanted to fish, but the water was high and muddy from the storm, so I decided to continue down. I walked slowly to enjoy this freedom, and when I came out of the mountains, I saw the sky over the prairie, and I thought that if heaven was real, I hoped it was a place I never had to go, because this earth was greater than any paradise.

July 6 Wednesday

I remember how powerful it was the first day I met Mayana. I had known love before and so was familiar not only with the power of the beginning, but also the power of the end. I was hesitant when I approached her because I had been hardened by the knowledge of my heart's ability to persuade my body to ignore my mind and dive in without any thoughts other than spontaneity. I had known love before, and so I recognized it when it was in front of me.

When we talked in a crowded barroom, the people around us were silenced, and I could only see her blue eyes. There was danger for me in the positioning of her hips, and I knew there would be no turning back once we exchanged phone numbers. I waited, as I believed I was supposed to, and tied up a few loose ends with other women I had been seeing before giving her a call.

We spent our first hours together hiking through

misty mountains beside a secluded river and discussing everything from the best vantage point to take a scenic photograph, to which side of a riffle is best to cast for trout. We traveled down bumpy two-tracks in my 1999 Jeep Cherokee and kept the windows open to feel the fresh air on our faces. When 3:00 p.m. arrived and I told her she had to drive because I had recently gotten a D.U.I. and my temporary license only allowed me to drive until this time on Saturdays, I believed she was impressed and thought of me as some form of sophisticated bad boy. If only she knew the rest, I thought. We decided to take roads I had never traveled, and for a while felt lost, but the sky was wide open and blue, so I navigated by the sun, directing her to turn down roads that were so remote there were no street signs, only cattle guards that rumbled under the wheels.

We came to a junction where the gravel crossed a paved road, and so turned east. Several miles down, we discovered a tavern and pulled in for a look. The barstools were the old red-padded, swivel sort, and I joked with her when her feet couldn't touch the floor. We drank a couple rounds of PBR while watching the Kentucky Derby on a small, old box television. I remember this distinctly because I had never watched the Derby before, and it seemed appropriate that it was on an old-fashioned TV set. She was excited and told me about her childhood. She was the oldest of five siblings, and each was born in a different state — one in another country. Her father was a wandering artist, so they moved frequently. One of her favorite memories was being young in Kentucky and raising hogs while living minimalistically. I didn't tell her too much of my past because I didn't want to scare her off, and it must have worked because when we found our way back to Casper, she invited me to see a concert with her that night. I have never been too much for live music, but it was in a small American Legion, and the crowd was exciting and the musicians energetic. There was no doubt we would see each other again, but when she left my house the next morning, I said something nonchalant, like, "It was nice knowing you." I've always found it perplexing that women are attracted to men who act distant and disinterested, and I still don't fully understand why. But that was okay. I had learned by then that what I didn't understand was nothing to shy away from, but rather it was what must be pursued.

...

I just paused from making this entry to go investigate the loud snap of a branch in the nearby forest. It must be around nine o'clock at night, judging by the deep blue-grey sky and the first few stars visible above. This is the time of night when most animals become active, and so I moved slowly through the forest towards the sound. I arrived in the approximate location but didn't see or hear anything. I knelt on a decaying ash tree and listened to the nighttime approach. Darkness carries a sound completely different than daylight. I had made up my mind to walk back to camp when the first wolf howled. He was near, but too far away to be what had caused me to get up and walk over. Within moments, there were several of them howling from a similar location, approximately three-hundred yards to my north. This forest became large and open to me, and I felt like I was made of tree and soil and animal flesh. For perhaps the first time in my life, I truly felt comfortable, and I knew I belonged here so definitely that any doubt I ever may have had became nonexistent. I felt the life of the soil beneath me, and I was in unison with the breathing of the trees and the magnetism of the moon.

I often think back to that first date with Mayana, and I wonder if other people have ever been so comfortable together while knowing so little about each other. I don't remember our second, or third, or really any other of our dates, but I remember the first one and the one that I proposed to her during. As was our theme, I proposed to her beside a mountainous trout stream in a place visited by fewer than one-hundred people per year, at the low end of a canyon where rattlesnakes and mountain lions were more frequent than humans. I had the ring in my pocket when I left her at camp to go fishing. I remember there being a light hatch of red Hexagenia on the river, and though I had an imitation that matched them nearly perfect, the fishing had been tough. Then I caught a nice rainbow trout that took me through a steep section of canyon between two sandstone cliffs, and I almost lost it in a beaver pond, but the hook set was true and I landed it a hundred yards downstream from where I had hooked it. I decided to keep it and take it to camp to fry over a fire. I thought Mayana would be swooned in some barbaric fashion, and that it would increase her attraction to me if I brought a live catch back to camp and gutted it before frying its delicate flesh.

We sat beside the fire and listened to coyotes yapping in the distant prairie. After eating the trout I asked her to marry me and she said no, she couldn't, because she was afraid to hurt me. I knew she didn't mean this, and let her juggle the thoughts in her head until they guided her to answer yes. I gave her a simple ring band because

I knew she was not drawn to the superfluous, and then we shared a bottle of Champagne while staying up late enough to watch the moon move from one side of the canyon to the other. I had known love before, and so I was familiar with the power of the beginning, and the power of the end, but I believed this was one that would not end. I felt immortal and confident, and after she fell asleep, I rekindled the fire and drank some beer while imagining all the mysterious life surrounding me in the darkness.

I didn't intend for this journal to become a memoir. It was my intention to keep it a factual representation of my daily activities here alone in the wild, but my mind does wander while in isolation, and I find relief by expressing these thoughts in the written form, even if nobody ever shall read them.

July 7 Thursday

I came to the forest not to think about the past, and not to escape it, but to find a new focus, a new discovery within myself. It seems the past hasn't really departed — it is still beside me, as if an adhesive attaches it to my shadow, and whenever I am in a silent moment it reminds me of its power over me. Rather than forget or ignore my past, I have decided to capture it, to be enraptured by it, and to explore it in the present tense. So I sit down and watch the trees to ease my mind. I have found a place where I can rest my eyes, and slow down this racing tract of time.

I will write my novel in the format of semi-autobiographical fiction. My life could be divided into segments, separate pieces like the limbs of a tree, and each limb could be studied not only for its current shape and condition, but also for the microcosmic events that designed it to be different than any other limb that has ever been created. I believe there is the material for at least one novel in every person, so for me, the difficult part has been determining which segment of my life to focus on. Since I am currently living in the wild, I will harness this present material and try to write about what has brought me to the wilderness.

I wish to create a protagonist separate from myself, but composed of the same desires and similar experiences. I want him to be better than me, but also to experience my pains and loves. I want him to be somebody I would want to know, but not too closely — like a favorite galaxy I enjoy watching through a telescope and studying in books, but one I will never visit. He should remain elusive by the very essence of being mysterious. I don't want to be him, for his pains and loves would be greater than I could take, but I want to watch him and grow from his experiences.

It is raining today which is okay because I spent the afternoon beneath the canopy and there were few mosquitoes present. There is a grey-green color to the forest when it rains, and despite popular opinion, I think this color is invigorating rather than depressing. This color highlights the living forest, and I can smell the ferns growing around me.

I am watching my rain barrels fill and there aren't any distractions in my mind. It is coming closer to the time that I must assemble my solar power system so I can begin the novel. I will not forget you, journal, but you will have to share my company with your technologically advanced counterpart. Tonight I will drink vodka and resort to the tent while I tie some flies and choose a new book to read. Tomorrow I must busy myself with further development of camp.

July 8 Friday

Tomorrow, tomorrow, there's always tomorrow. I am a procrastinator by design. I remember when I was in the fifth grade, and my teacher handed out awards to the students at the end of the school year. These were not competitive awards, because every student got one, but rather they were personal achievement awards. One of my classmates got the best at math, another was best on the monkey bars. My good friend at the time was awarded the best penmanship. So when the teacher handed me my envelope, I was rich with anticipation. I opened it to discover a word that was unfamiliar to me, and so I assumed it was a mistake but decided to wait until the teacher had handed out the rest of the awards before mentioning it to him. Teacher, I said, what does *procrastinator* mean? He said it was a unique award that he had never given to any of his students in the twenty years he'd been teaching. This filled me with pride, and I wanted to ask him more, but decided to wait until I got home and ask my parents. When my mother explained the definition to me, I realized how wise and observant my teacher had been. She said this was not a compliment, and that she would have a talk with my teacher the next morning. I went to my room and thought about it some more. I realized I was a procrastinator, by choice. For me, the word described someone patient and studious and willing to wait for the best possible solution, rather than someone who acted with haste. So I am a procrastinator, and today I will not begin my novel, but rather, I will spend time wandering through the forest in my own thoughts, and studying the members of this biotic community that are new to me. There is a novel hidden in these trees, and I will discover it.

Earlier today I knelt beside a bunchberry plant and

studied the stems rising up from the center, which had begun to produce fruit. I looked closer and saw smaller life forms moving on the leaves. Then I noticed something large on the underside of one of the leaves. It was so obvious I wondered how it was not the first thing I noticed. It wasn't even well camouflaged, but its deep grey color and absolute stillness kept it hidden from me. I opened my guidebook for the moths and butterflies of Minnesota and learned that this was a sphinx moth. I read about its life cycle and biological design, but mostly I was impressed by its freedom. Not an easy life, certainly, to be born in the forest, to have such a short lifespan, and to be hunted by birds and weasels and other insects. But to be free, absolutely free, and only governed by the immediate desire to survive — that was what impressed me most.

There were many wood ticks on my legs when I returned to camp. I started a fire and then peeled them from my skin and flicked them in, one by one. If I listened closely, I could hear a faint squeal when they ignited. I imagined this was their final scream before a fiery death, and I was pleased. Perhaps I am being unfair by admiring the life of a moth and so easily destroying the life of a wood tick. Doesn't each deserve the same opportunity to survive? Maybe so, but if the moth had latched onto my flesh, I surely would have smacked it dead without a second thought.

It was getting dark and the sky was cloudless above me. Many stars burned above, but I could only watch them for a short while before I was struck by a vicious anxiety at the realization of my smallness. I am smaller than the moth and even less valuable to Earth than the wood tick. The stars know nothing of me, and though I may know a little about their existence, they are completely indescribable to my limited knowledge. So much vastness in the sky, and I have never even been to the bottom of the ocean.

I threw several large logs onto the fire because I knew I would stay up late. There were deer and bear and wolves in the dark forest around me, and I wondered if they have ever wondered about the stars. Is the mind of mankind our greatest asset, or is the curse of a conscience a confused mind? If I were to remove the thoughts that were larger than my own self, the thoughts that were not required for my survival, and clear my head of the philosophical wonderings, would I be any more happy and content? If I were one with the moment and unconcerned with anything larger, would I not become greater in size by comparison? Can man ever be happy while his thirst for knowledge is unquenched?

I grew tired of these circular questions, so I poured my first vodka Tang of the night, and pulled my chair closer to the fire. If happiness required me to ignore my thoughts and questions, then I hoped to never be happy. It is greater to have doubts and uncertainties because they keep me guessing and examining, and I do believe that is why I am alive.

When I called Mayana today, she expressed an interest in staying home this weekend and not coming to the property. She said her week had been so busy that she needed a couple days alone to rest, and that the drive to work next Monday morning would be treacherous. I gave her my consent, even though I was looking forward to her company. This will be the first time in my life I have gone two entire weeks without seeing another human being. This will be a test of my sanity and preparation, and I look forward to it.

I have enough supplies at camp to survive several weeks, so this does not concern me, but I will have to ration my vodka. I have enough food, but diversity is minimal. All that remains are Clif bars, canned food, and dried pasta. This is not too bad, but I do look forward to the fresh brats and the bottle of wine she brings on her weekend visits. Perhaps this will inspire me to spend more effort fishing.

July 9 Saturday

The rain is heavy tonight and with each bolt of lightning my small electric lantern flickers. The lantern I use is a compact collapsible model with LED bulbs that runs on four AAA batteries. This, along with my headlamp, which runs on two AAA batteries (both of which are currently dead), and my cell phone, are the only electrical items I have at camp. The cell phone is off all day except during the five to ten minutes I spend talking to Mayana each night when I walk to the end of my two-track.

The lantern doesn't do much more than illuminate a small enough area to see this notebook. Behind me, in the darkness of this tent, I can barely see the white of Sly's fur. Outside of the screen windows, there is nothing except shadows. Then the lightning strikes, and for a brief second I can see the shapes of the forest, but the shapes are deceptive, and it is dark again before I have identified them. When the darkness returns, I feel the fear. Not a mental fear, because my mind is clear with the belief that I could defeat any threat this forest would present, but a physical fear, the type I feel in my shoulders — the type I have known in the past that preluded combat. This is when I unsheathe my knife and set it on the desk beside this notebook in the small light. When the lightning strikes again and briefly illuminates the forest, my imagination searches for all the dangers that could be lurking in the black. Despite all my reasoning and common sense, there is no way to eliminate a fear of the dark while alone in the wild.

I just thought of a quote that I believe is credited to John Wayne: "Courage is being scared to death, and saddling up anyway." Well I have no horse here to saddle, but I will not run, I will not leave and seek the comfort of light switches and company. I am here by choice, and I will master this fear.

Even inside of my tent, I have no peripheral vision. All that exists around me is darkness. Darkness is more powerful than light because it is more mysterious. I try to avoid looking into the darkness because what I cannot see is more frightful than what I can. If I had a large spotlight in front of my tent, and in that light was illuminated a dozen cougars, twenty wolves, and five large bears, I would not fear them. It is the act of wondering what is there in the dark that causes fear.

July 10 Sunday

I am more surprised by the cold of night than by the hot of day. The temperature must have reached upper eighties today, with humidity levels in the same range, and I was sweating while sitting in the shade. Tonight I am cold. I had a fire earlier but the mosquitoes were bad and the smoke was no deterrent, so I came into the tent where there are fewer of them. Their buzzing screams echo around these canvas walls, and I am constantly swatting the empty air.

If I had to guess the temperature tonight, I would say low fifties. This doesn't sound too bad at first, but my judgment is skewed from all the years spent living in a house with heat and proper insulation. Here in the forest with nothing but the cold and stale air around me, I shiver in the darkness. I pull my fleece blanket from the bed and wrap it around my shoulders as I sit at the desk to make this entry. All of my exposed skin feels numb and my legs shiver slightly. I think about the nights in Wyoming that I spent camping in snow caves high in the mountains, and I thought this contrast would make me feel warm, but I am only reminded of the snow and the icicles that formed on my beard, and my imagination is transported into those freezing conditions.

So I let it ride. I let myself feel the pain. I have felt it before and survived. I have felt it worse and the next day I was stronger. I will tolerate this and tomorrow the sun will shine on my face and the muggy air will make me wish for cold.

Earlier today, while sitting in my own sweat, I thought back to the summer of 1999. That was the first summer I spent working as a professional drywall carpenter, and the season had been exceptionally hot. There were heat advisory warnings and stories on the news of the people who had died from heat exhaustion. We didn't let that stop us. I was part of a three-man crew working on high scaffolding in new construction without air conditioning or fans. I was drinking several gallons of Gatorade a day to stay hydrated, and I still felt lightheaded many times. None of us complained, and none of us expressed interest in taking the day off. We were all too proud and so couldn't be the first to suggest this for fear of sounding weak. We did our job and kept each other strong by suppressing our own discomforts. I look back on it now and am proud for not backing down, for doing my job and not letting discomforts sway me. I am glad to have that memory, and to know there was a time in my life when I was tested in those conditions. I hope the future holds new tests and I continue to be willing to face them.

July 11 Monday

The air was calm and heavy with mosquitoes, and the orange sunset was on the water when the structure of my life was decided. Not to imply the intricate future and sequence of events were predestined, for I would be as capricious as every other living entity, but the night I learned to fly fish created in me a beacon that would guide my decisions and offer me sanctuary for as long as I shall live. I was thirteen years old, and waded out in shorts and bare feet onto the mucky bottom of the lake. There were fish splashing on the surface all around me. My father stood on the shore to watch and offer me direction. I attached a mosquito impression he had tied earlier that night, and he talked me through the casting technique. Pumpkinseed sunfish were spawning, and so they were swollen and prolific. Wherever my fly landed, it was promptly attacked, and all I had to do was set the hook. The lightweight fly rod made these fish into great fighters, and I caught many.

It was that night that I became a fly angler, and though I strayed from that path and went by many other titles during my years of rebellion and self-searching through the jungles of youth, I had it in my source-blood, and I knew that wherever my life took me, that night would always be vivid and present. After I escaped from the turmoil of youth and began to search for peace of mind with a fly rod, I always imagined my father standing on the shore beside me, and every cast I made was with the intention of impressing him and showing him that he had taught me well.

Earlier today, I put on my waders and took my fly rod to the river to cast for muskie. The water was slow-moving and deep amber in color. I saw the trees reflected on the water, and heard the birds chirping, and spent many moments thinking before making my first cast. I used a Deceiver pattern that I had tied this morning to match the color of baitfish I have seen in this river. I made long casts using a sinking line and let my fly swim in a wide arc on the deep side of a riffle.

On the shore behind me, I felt the presence of my father, uncle, and grandfather. They watched and commented amongst themselves, but said nothing to me. I took this as a sign that I had graduated from the stage of pupil and had been elevated to the status of equal, of a man they could watch and admire, and even though they may disagree with certain of my techniques and decisions, they respected me enough to allow my own method without their influence.

I caught no fish, but spent several great hours casting and imagining their presence with me. When I returned to camp, they walked behind me on the trail, and we said not a word about getting skunked today, but rather, spoke of the times we returned from the water with a stringer full of fish, and how we filleted them and left the guts out for bears and eagles, and how those fish tasted fresh when we fried them over a fire.

When I sat beside the fire alone tonight, I thought of all the devious and disgraceful deeds I have done in my day, and I was glad that the presence of my father, uncle, and grandfather were not with me then, that they only share my time when I fish, and that I can count on them to be with me during my best. Perhaps they are with me always, but I ignore them while engaged in the devious. This is ironic, because I am certain they have participated in their share of the devious. But not like me, I am certain of that.

July 12 Tuesday

If time travel were possible, I would set the dial on whatever machine I traveled by and force it to always repeat today. Nothing too profound or magnificent occurred, but what I learned was that a regular day alone in the woods is better than any day in any city with any company. This may sound outlandish or misanthropic, but I am certain the human mind was designed for solitude. I love the people in my life and cherish our time spent together, but I realized that on a subliminal level I have always been distracted by them. I want to be able to hear my own thoughts and live in my own daydreams. I want to be able to make the world up as I go. I want to be free to decide who I am without trying to be who they want me to be. Perhaps this is juvenile, and as an adult, I should embrace the sacrifice required to be part of the living organism that is society. I am capable of doing so, and I have proved this to myself many times, but every time I feel less whole, as if that sacrifice has depreciated the value of my life, has carved out a little piece of my individuality, and left me slightly more hollow and less interesting. Conformity is about the least interesting attribute I can imagine in a person, and the great hypocrisy is that this attribute is required if a person wants to be successful.

So, if time travel were possible, I would repeat today, or yesterday, or any day that I have spent alone in wild places. I would carry the memory of people who have left their impressions on me, and I would wish they were as happy as I, but I would not wish them to be here with me now. Find your own solitude to discover your hidden thoughts and think of me often, as I will you.

July 13 Wednesday

When I talked to Mayana on the phone tonight, she said that her dad had become ill, and she sounded extremely worried. I told her I would drive home to be with her, that it wouldn't matter to miss a couple nights in the forest since I had all summer, but she insisted I stay. She said that at the end of summer I would regret it if I hadn't spent the entire season in the wild, and that she would be okay. There was nothing I could do to change her father's condition. I thought this was brave of her and I knew she didn't mean it. I knew that she needed someone to tell her everything was all right. So I hung up the phone and packed a small bag to travel to town.

I got to my Jeep and it wouldn't start. This frustrated me so I tried to fix it. The battery was dead, so I carried the fifty pound deep-cycle battery that would be used for my solar power from camp to the Jeep. I tried jumping the Jeep battery with this deep-cycle battery, but it had not been charged because I had yet to assemble my solar power system. I was upset because I wanted to be with her but there was nothing I could do short of walking the eighty-five miles to town.

I tried to call her again but could get no reception beneath the approaching storm clouds, so I walked back to camp and made this entry. After thinking about it for a while, I decided that this forest does not want me to leave, and I belong to her now.

July 14 Thursday

It is quiet in the forest tonight, and I am alone in my canvas tent. I had thought about calling Mayana, so I collected my cell phone and walked up the dark trail towards the road, but the phone battery was dead, so I returned to camp with this notebook for company. I have been charging the battery in the Jeep while letting the engine run, but the Jeep's battery is dead, so I won't be able to use my phone again until I assemble the solar power system.

...

It is easy for this silence to provoke my memory of the previous life, of the life that others still live in their cities. I walk outside into the darkness and sit on the soil beside my tent. In this peace, I can see clearly the places I have been and the people who are there still. The lonely men who sit at barstools swapping stories of glory while staring aimlessly at a television set, hoping the bar won't ever close because their beds are too empty but here there is company. The single women walking in high heels on concrete to the places where lonely men gather, and their hopes of being noticed, of acquiring attention, of feeling needed and allowing themselves to need somebody. Of the dreams and aspirations that everyone shares but are spoken of as if a foreign language when we try to communicate. The families in their houses with their dogs sleeping and their babies crying out for a midnight teat. The lovers so engrossed by their company that the entire world melts away with the power of their passion. The sirens on the streets and the criminals sleeping on the floor of a cell beside a stranger who for tonight is their best friend. The working people trying to find sleep before the alarm clock screams them awake and they put on a false face to enter a new day. The quiet neighborhoods where children play in the grass and parents wait for bedtime so they can experience a moment of respite. All those happy and discontented people in the world and I am alone. I love my silence and my solitude, and I live in my memory of other people's lives. I feel the power of their existence and I am lost in my attempts to understand them.

I hear the wings of bats above me, and the mosquitoes buzz in my ears. Around my periphery, I see the flickering green of fireflies. In the darkness not far away, the crackle of branches beneath the weight of a larger animal. If I could look into my own eyes right now, that face would be of a stranger, and I would want to be him. I see the faces of people I used to know but they look the same as ever, and I don't think they would recognize me. I love my solitude and the way the forest smells after dark, and I am happy with the life I have made here in the trees, but I know some day they will see me again. Someday I will again have to wonder what they want me to be, and I will be forced to accommodate to the best of my ability if I am to survive and make a success in their world. It may be the most difficult part of living, trying to fulfill the expectations of the people in our lives.

July 15 Friday

The contemplative man always lives alone. Regardless of who may reside in his home, his is a solitary world. There have been many roommates in my past — some family, some friends or acquaintances, some strangers, some lovers — but I was always separated from them by an invisible force that kept us resigned to the worlds of our own thoughts. So this solitude in the forest is nothing new to me. Being alone in my thoughts is how I have always been, but this is the first time I have lived physically alone for twenty-four hours a day, day after day.

I did not take the company of others for granted, even though I may never have expressed an appreciation for them. I valued their proximity because I enjoyed having somebody else to look at and wonder about. Watching them provided an escape from my mind while I simultaneously dug deeper into it. I listened to them speak and watched them act out the lives of the characters they chose to be, but I rarely engaged. I was a spectator and preferred they knew little of me. It's amazing how most people will entirely ignore the topic of somebody else if given the opportunity to speak about themselves. I listened, and I knew someday I would utilize this information for future fictional writings. I studied them and let them speak, and I lived my own life and gained my own experiences, but kept these internal. I had the opinion that it would be greater to save my thoughts and let them grow, and since I was never very good at expressing them verbally, I would wait until the clarity came and then try to write them. This usually came in the form of poetry, and I have shoeboxes full of scribbled pages in verse and rhyme.

Trying to express these thoughts is frustrating because I must sharpen my pencil after every couple sentences; not that I have much better to do this time of night. Today I was busy occupying unproductive time. I spent much time pacing back and forth through camp, occasionally stopping to study the shape of a tree or search for a bird that I could hear but could not see. I sat on the log beside the river for many hours, and though my thoughts were always full, they resulted in no profound discoveries. Perhaps that is the greatest discovery of all — finding a place to think without any requirement for a resolution.

It is a calm and quiet night. I imagine the silent animals in the dark forest, and I can feel their eyes watching me. I keep the fire dim in an attempt to bring the animals closer, and I must angle this notebook down towards its light so I can see clearly to write. I feel the darkness behind me and it weighs heavily with unknowns.

I am no longer certain of my belief that sasquatch are fictional, and I even consider the viability of wild clans of humans who have remained hidden in these forests for centuries and are now creeping silently behind me. They are most likely cannibals, and this is why their presence remains unknown — because they eat all witnesses. These thoughts seem absurd as I write them, but the imagination is a powerful creature, and its power grows the longer it is left alone. I am not afraid, but I am aware that there are things I don't understand, and that the forest is filled with mysteries.

July 16 Saturday

Today I will assemble my camp shower. It's been over three weeks since I last took a shower, though every day I either bathe in the river, stand beneath a cleansing rain, or dip a soapy sponge into one of my rain barrels to wash with. There was a time in my life when I showered twice a day, every morning and every night. It wasn't because I was a clean freak or germaphobe — rather, I enjoyed the sensation of standing in hot water and feeling it permeate my skin. The shower design I have in mind for camp will not reproduce that sensation, but I've got a pretty good plan that should approximate it and, at the very least, keep me clean. I'm going to set down this notebook, finish my cup of coffee, then get to it.

...

I finished the job and my shower looks ready for use. I cut a small hole, about one inch in diameter, at the center bottom of a five-gallon pail. This alone could have worked, I would fill the bucket with water and then stand beneath the drain. But, being that I am a human, I wanted something more complex and inventive. I considered my options for making a showerhead. I rummaged through all of my supplies, but there was nothing that jumped out as perfect. Then I noticed a pair of socks hanging up on the clothesline to dry. I had an idea.

I cut a strip of nylon tarp about two feet long and eight inches wide. I rolled it up into a tube like a hose and wrapped it with a good layer of duct tape. I then took a sock from the line, inserted the hose down to where my ankles would be if wearing it, and fastened that with duct tape. To bond the hose to the bucket I used the epoxy that came with a tent patching kit and smeared the epoxy all around the bottom hole in the bucket and along the part of hose that would be inserted. I then inserted the hose and bonded them together. This seemed essentially watertight. I finished it off by placing a mosquito net over the top to keep out larger debris.

After letting the epoxy cure, it was time to test it. I chose a small clearing on the north side of camp and fastened a section of polybraid rope between two balsam fir trees, about eight feet up. At the center of that line, I tied a two-foot section of rope and then tied a carabiner clip to the bottom end where I could attach the handle of my shower bucket. I filled up my bucket about three-quarters full with rainwater and attached it. Water came squirting out through the sock and I was knelt beneath it to wash. It was extremely cold, but there was a greater discomfort — the mosquitoes swarmed to my wet, naked flesh. I washed and rinsed as quickly as possible, all the while cursing the buzzing beasts and swatting them from the air and off my skin. Thinking of it now, I must have been quite the spectacle, and I can only imagine the laughs I would have received should anyone have been watching from the trees.

July 17 Sunday

My eyes burn and the fumes irritate my nose. When I inhale, my lungs want to reject this air. My skin feels like I am submersed in an incendiary vapor. Citronella was designed to repel mosquitoes, but it would do a pretty good job of repelling humans as well.

Sly managed to slide open the zipper to my tent earlier today, and I didn't notice until coming in to bed, so the mosquitoes are abundant inside tonight. I lit two citronella candles as fumigants and let them burn with the door shut while I sat by the fire, but the mosquitoes were intolerable outside, so I reentered the tent and extinguished one of the candles while the other still burns as I write this entry. The mosquitoes buzz and scream and prick at my flesh. No matter how many of them I murder in a bloody rage, their comrades are not deterred. They are kamikaze soldiers and no death can dissuade them. But they will not win.

It was a fine day and I had an idea for how to start my novel, but I will not go into detail now because my thoughts are distracted by the mosquitoes. They are the masters of this forest. It is not that I am unwanted here by them, but rather they cherish my presence the way I would cherish a freshly baked pizza being delivered to camp. I am spending more time swatting the air and smacking them on my skin than I am writing, so I will cover myself with sleeping bags and try to sleep.

July 18 Monday

If you're going to be a small fish, the least you can do is be a big fighter.

Today I walked up to the road and headed east to where the river crosses beneath a bridge. I was only a mile and a half upstream from camp, but it felt like a different world. Here the river was fast and shallow as it cut around boulders through a sharp riffle. This was much different than the slow, placid surface of my shoreline. Behind me was the occasional sound of motor vehicles pounding across the bridge, and the rhythm of their tires echoed in reverberations through the river corridor. It certainly was not a busy street, averaging about one car every fifteen to twenty minutes, but it was more human interference than I had encountered since arriving at camp roughly a month ago. I turned my back to the bridge and waded to the upstream side of the riffle where the water was deeper, and I began casting muskie flies.

The fishing was easy, but this wasn't because I was catching any fish. It was easy because the sound of the bridge was muted by the volume of the riffle between us, and with my back to the bridge, I could see only a pristine river that sliced through a corridor of cedars, spruce, and alders. It was easy because the sun was bright and hot, but there was a gentle breeze that kept me cool and comfortable. It was easy because the river was wide and I enjoyed making long casts and watching my line shoot out and unfurl gently on the surface. It was easy because there was nothing else I should be doing.

I was casting a fly six inches long, constructed of grizzly hackle, marabou, magnum strips, and cactus chenille, with barbell eyes for weight, so when I felt the fish, I knew it must be large. It was a violent strike that happened at the beginning of my retrieve, so there was roughly sixty feet of line between us. The fish pulled hard and dove towards the deep center of the channel before swimming upstream.

I followed him into a deep pool and tried to stay shallow enough to prevent water from spilling into the top of my chest waders. This was going well until I tripped over a submerged log and the river poured in. I didn't let this bother me, but kept my line tight and the fish was still attached. He was deep so I was fighting not only his strength, but also the weight of water between us. It was more than just a physical battle — it had become a battle of wits. The fish believed it would tire me by holding to the bottom, and it must have known that I could not follow it there. I got parallel to its position with only thirty feet of line between us. I knew the hook set was good, so I began to pull. Slowly the fish came towards me as I inched towards it. The water was sliding over my waders when the fish got another idea and began to circle me. I held my rod vertical and rotated with it like a carousel. He bolted to the shallows and hid behind a boulder, so I got in behind him and reeled up my slack line. I was close enough now that I should have seen him. As I gave another tug on my line and raised the rod tip, a ten-inch smallmouth bass leapt from the river in front of me. I knew this couldn't be the fish that had put up such a forceful effort, so I presumed it was rushing away from the monster muskie that was on my hook. I had seen similar things happen while fishing.

I saw my fly line trailing the fish as it splashed back into the river. I was both disappointed and impressed. I reeled in line fast and held my net beneath the surface. The fish rushed towards me, and as I swept at it, the net grazed my line and released the hook from the fish's tail. My line went slack and I stood in wet befuddlement. As I walked back to camp, and listened to the water splash inside my waders, I decided it was the fight I would remember, and I was pleased to have encountered such an opponent.

July 19 Tuesday

It was a cool damp morning when I rose from the tent and took a walk through the forest. I left Sly at camp, and wandered through the trees to my south. I came upon a clearing beneath tall Elm trees. Here the undergrowth was minimal, with a few ferns and columbine. There was a deer standing on the far side. It was a young buck who must have been aware of my presence, because he stood perfectly still half-hidden by a small fir tree. I stood and watched him for a while. I was most likely the first human he had ever seen. I wondered what he thought of me, and if there was an instinctual fear. I suppose, like humans, animals are subject to fearing what they don't understand.

Eventually I took a step towards him, to see how close I could get. This was a game he did not want to play, and promptly galloped into the forest. I continued in the direction he went, and came upon a narrow trail that went east towards the river. I walked down the trail and encountered wolf scat that was so fresh it was steaming in the cool air. I wanted to see the wolf and knew it was likely nearby, so I knelt down and waited for a sound.

It was my mother who taught me an appreciation for wild animals. I remember the house where we lived in the woods beside a lake, and she was always excited when wildlife came through our yard. She had a profound kindness when it came to these animals, and I sensed she would have done anything to keep them safe. The animal kingdom was not to be feared or conquered, but a populace that deserved our admiration and respect. There was mystery in their way of life, and as domesticated humans, the closest we could come to our roots was to watch and learn from these animals who spent their entire lives at the mercy of nature. This made them truly grand and accomplished individuals, and if we remained compassionate and humble, then we might understand.

I remained knelt down on the trail for quite some time, and then continued to the river. When I got to the water, I followed the shore back to camp. I thought about my own roots, and wondered if I had been young in a city instead of a forest, would I ever have come to this place. I believe there is a connection to wild places in all of us, and it is created by compassion and wonder for what has been lost.

July 20 Wednesday

We are a species that lives in our imagination. I've always believed this was true, and I've seen it not only in myself, but also in others. I've watched them try to make sense of the world where they walked even though their minds roamed through another place. I have felt empathy for their journey because it was one that I knew also. There are as many versions of the world as there are eyes to see it, but I just now wondered for the first time if animals counted in that same populace.

I watched a squirrel near camp today who seemed braver than most. He got close as I sat in the screen house, and he worked the forest floor in zigzags searching for food. There was another squirrel fifty feet away who would not get close, and this one worked the forest floor in circles. I wondered about the design of their methods and realized each one had learned from its own experiences which method worked best. This required imagination, for imagination is the ability to develop an idea sourced from the reality that one has perceived. These two squirrels were of the same species, born and raised in the proximal forest, but were of separate minds. Perhaps I am stretching this a bit, as the squirrel's brain is small, and we credit imagination to brain capacity; but if humans only use one-tenth of our brains, isn't that roughly the size of a squirrels?

Maybe I have been alone too long. Maybe I am searching for entertainment through unrealistic reaches of my imagination. But if I can imagine it, then there must be some connection to reality.

July 21 Thursday

It has been two weeks since Mayana's previous visit. It has been two weeks since anyone has seen my face. It has been two weeks since I have looked into the face of another human being. I am alone, and doing well.

It has been good, and living on this minimal supply of food makes me feel strong and lean. I know that if

I were alone in a city for this long, I would have spent more time eating extravagantly. Here I am never bored. Here I never feel like I need more. This is everything for me and that is enough.

There has been a change in my mentality. There is something entirely new in the way I view the world. What I see is completely mine for there has been nobody to influence me otherwise. I have built a vision that is entirely my own. I wonder how long it will take after being submersed in civilization to regain that ubiquitous view of the world. I wonder if I will always remember the serenity of having nothing else to believe but my own opinion. I am alone, and I am happy.

July 22 Friday

When I am with her, I wonder how I ever thought I was so happy alone. When I see her through the trees gathering kindling for a fire, I understand why men decided to build homes and start a family. When Mayana is at camp, this forest becomes brighter.

As is generally the case, I stay awake beside the fire long after she has fallen asleep. Tonight she sleeps curled up on the soil beside me, with her feet near the flames and her head resting on my coat, which is folded into a pillow. Our day was filled with blooming flowers and singing birds. There were spiders, mosquitoes, and wood ticks, as there always are, but they did not bother us. We squeezed our bodies through the thick foliage, tethered together by our hands, and tried to get lost in this forest. When we came to a small clearing where the sun penetrated the canopy beneath a tall old ash tree, we took a moment to sit and sip a cup of coffee.

We got engaged this past April while camping in the

Medicine Bow Mountains of Wyoming, after I returned to camp with a fresh trout from Deer Creek, and we decided then that we would wait until after my time in the woods to get married. We agreed that it would be best to wait until we both were established in new careers, and that we would not rush because it was the rest of our lives, and it didn't make any difference if there were a piece of paper to prove it. Today, in the shade of the trees and the serenity of being entirely alone in our own wilderness, we changed the plan.

There was no reason to wait, and having a career proved nothing. Anybody can get a career, but only the romantically inclined can find a love like ours. So, in the honor of romance, we decided to move our plans for a wedding to this coming autumn. That's in two months. Despite my assuredness that both Mayana and I are perfectly capable and willing to live alone during that time and plan our wedding, my fundamental sense of responsibility kicked in tenfold while making this entry—I am unemployed with no income. Shouldn't a man who's getting married be a provider? Even in today's world where the woman may likely make more money, shouldn't he still contribute? I was plagued with an emotion that I wouldn't call guilt or doubt, but something else that could only have been derived from my father, a man whose foremost determination was to provide for his family.

Setting the commitment for being a provider aside, should I not be there with her? If we are to be married in two months, is it unfair of me to be living alone in the forest? If it were any other woman, I would say yes. If it were any other woman, I wouldn't be secure enough with her to be here. If it were any other woman, I wouldn't be confident that she understands me being here is a prerequisite for being myself. I am a fortunate man, for I am afraid many men marry for much less.

July 23 Saturday

We woke early this morning with plans to go canoeing. When we arrived at the river, we decided instead to spend some time clearing up our canoe launching sight. The foliage had become long and thick, the ground was pocketed with muskrat holes, and a large piece of driftwood had anchored directly in front of the shore. I retrieved my machete and let Mayana work at clearing the foliage while I slipped into the river and began to relocate the driftwood. It was soft and heavy from being waterlogged, and I found myself wishing to use a chainsaw. Instead, I located a recently felled spruce with a diameter roughly six inches and used it as leverage to guide the driftwood out into the current. This only partially worked, but I was able to secure it at an angle out from our shore that would allow passage by canoe.

We both worked diligently, and neither of us spoke of our new plans to be married this autumn. I could sense that Mayana was working out plans in her head, and that the glow of her face was from more than the simple pleasure of spending time outdoors. There was an inkling of consternation around the corner of her eyes, and I interpreted this to be caused by her considering the same difficulties of our plan that I had been. I have known people married under much less optimal conditions, and some of them were even successful, but these difficulties would be ours and we had no playbook for reference or guidance. This certainly wasn't the way I thought it would be when I was young and imagined myself emulating my parents' life. Even though their marriage ultimately ended in divorce, I still carried with me the idea that the old-fashioned way of marrying, with the man being a provider for the woman who was a mother and housekeeper, and the structure of designated roles, was the way a monogamous relationship should be. I have encountered a paradigm shift, and that is one of the many powers love has. I will stay in the forest past the date of our wedding, I will be a married man living alone in the wild, and when I return to her and the world made by men, I will work hard and make a life for us. Wherever I am living and whatever job I may end up with after this adventure, I am not worried and I believe we have the best story that I know of in real life.

July 24 Sunday

When I woke up this morning, Mayana had coffee and bacon ready. It is a difficult and insipid life I live here in the forest. The smell of bacon is almost as satisfying as the taste, and Sly was possibly more excited than I. After eating nearly the full pound of bacon, I poured the grease from the pan onto some dog food in his dish, and he spent an hour licking the dish dry while Canyon circled him, hoping for leftovers. He reminded me of a hyena circling a lion who was consuming a fresh kill.

The dogs spent most of the day chasing squirrels while Mayana and I read in the screen house and shared passages that struck us as powerful. My favorite line was from *Lord Jim*, by Joseph Conrad: "A man that is born falls into a dream like a man who falls into the sea." If I weren't a wilderness man, I would likely be a seaman. The vastness of the ocean contains solitude like no other place, but I would miss the trees. I would miss the solid earth and the sight of animals. Mostly I would miss the sound of wolves howling.

Last night we stayed by the fire until late, and after lying in bed, we heard the wolves howling in the forest nearby. They were closer than I have heard them before, and this was exciting. The thought of wolves living in the same forest as me makes this little wilderness feel wilder. If it were not for the wolves, I would not have selected this location for my adventure. To me they are the definition of wilderness. I have been in the presence of wild wolves many times, but have only seen several of them. It is their illusory nature that makes them mysterious. It is their mystery that makes them coveted.

I sit beside the river now, and listen to its motion. The water here flows slowly, as if dragging the anchor of its own weight. It drags the land with it as it goes, taking some away, and depositing some new. In the silence of a calm day I can hear this shifting of the land, and it is much different than the sounds of riffles I am used to in the mountains. I hear it push and pull, and I know that though the surface looks undisturbed, there are infinite changes happening below.

Mayana drove home tonight instead of waking early for the drive tomorrow. I charged my phone in her car before she left so I can call her this week. The previous two weeks without her went by quickly, but the next week alone seems like an eternity. I am ready for it, and I am ready to write.

July 25 Monday

It's been many days since I've watched television, listened to the radio, or surfed the web. I've always enjoyed movies and music, and so I thought their absence would be difficult, but I miss them none. Maybe music some. I have no connection to the outside world except for Mayana, and the only news she shares with me is of the personal type. I do not know what is going on in the world out there, and that is fine. I do not know what sports teams are winning or what's playing at the theatre. I do not know of the weather in Asia or of the wars in the Middle East. I do not know what new coffee shops have opened in town or which of my neighbors are keeping their yards mowed. For all I know the President could be dead — or worse, Bob Dylan. What I do not know presents new space for new knowledge, and what I do know is all that matters to me here.

What I know is that the leaves of trees are quieter in the morning and this presents an auditorium for the birds to sing. What I know is that the splash of a fish in the river can be heard at camp on a gentle night. What I know is the musty smell of my canvas tent after a rain. What I know is that there are far more species of plants and animals in this forest than I could ever understand. What I know is that the ferns respond to the mildest of breezes, and their delicate leaves pulse and wiggle like fingers playing a piano. What I know is that the smallest animals fear me less than the larger ones. What I know is that being alone doesn't have to be lonely. What I know is that the new knowledge I learn cannot expunge the memories of my past.

I also know that I must write. In the absence of societal distractions, I have discovered a greater desire to produce, to create, and to express myself. I do not know if my abilities are good, but I do know that I must use them. I do know that if I were to live a life without writing, my head would be too full at the end, and that I would have shared nothing. What I know now is more than what I knew before, and there is still much time ahead.

July 26 Tuesday

I would like to discuss the animal tracks I have seen today, but I must be brief, for the sky is shedding the sun and my brat is about to burn. At all the locations where the trails enter camp, I have seen the tracks of a large deer. Around the south side of camp, I have seen the tracks of a medium-sized varmint too obscure to identify but is likely a larger member of the weasel family. On my walk to the river, I saw a bear track slightly larger than my palm.

The brat is ready. I should've brought ketchup. I will eat my brat and feed Sly his, and then go rinse Sly's dog dish in the river. Tonight I will remain by my fire until the logs burn out and then retreat to my tent where I will do some reading.

...

There is a faint light remaining in the sky and the fire is burning hot, so I will jot down a few more thoughts. It is getting late and I have had a few vodka Tangs, but I will make one final note: my dog just killed a frog. I wish he hadn't, not because I have any sort of prejudice towards the life of a frog, but because frogs eat mosquitoes, and I certainly have a prejudice against them. I think we need to retain any life form that helps devour these bloodthirsty beasts. How do I communicate this fact to Sly?

Firewood is low and the air is black ten feet from the radius of this fire. There was a beeping in my pocket, and I dug in to find my cell phone still turned on from my call to Mayana. It beeped to indicate the battery was dying; it goes quickly if turned on here in the woods where it is constantly roaming. This worried me briefly, thinking of the phone calls I would miss and how detached I would be without my phone. Then I remembered I am in the forest and it is the city which makes us feel detached. I turned it off and will now retreat to the tent where there is a book waiting for me.

July 27 Wednesday

Today was quite productive; however, so much can happen in a day that I have no realistic intention of discussing it all here in this journal. So let this be a summary of notes.

Today I installed the solar power system. I mounted the panels on a table approximately four feet high, which I built with natural lumber and a couple remaining 2X4's. The panels are connected to a charge controller, which regulates power flow to the battery. The battery is a 12-volt, deep-cycle, commercial-grade monstrosity that weighs over eighty pounds, and which I was told, in tandem with a dozen others, could power an entire television station for twenty-four hours. The battery then runs through a pure sine wave 350-watt charge inverter, allowing the DC solar power to be used with any AC appliance. Charging my laptop and cell phone are the only uses I will have for it. I am writing this daily journal in a notebook by hand, but I will also be writing the novel, for which I will use my laptop.

It's getting dark so that's all for today. One final note. I spent thirty to forty-five minutes casting my fly rod this afternoon to no resulting catch. Before summer ends, I will dedicate more time to the pursuit of hooking a fish from this river.

Final final note. I have never seen such a dense swarm of mosquitoes as when I was preparing to enter the tent for sleep. They were a smog surrounding Sly that I had to fight off before quickly opening the tent and rushing him in. I'm sure that the forest has never seen a man strip so quickly while swatting his way into a tent. No outside clothes get worn inside the tent because there may be wood ticks attached to them. The clouds blowing low above the trees look like it's going to rain. The mosquitoes are the storm before the storm.

July 28 Thursday

It's difficult for me to write here tonight. I spent all of today writing fifteen pages of my novel. That's the first addition of many more. I'm glad I got a good start today, for the delay of settling into camp has made me distracted. I also made mental notes for future scenes I would like to write. I have a scene in mind that I will sleep on tonight and write tomorrow.

It has been cool, cloudy, and relatively windy all day, threatening to rain. The first few raindrops fell as I picked up this journal. It has paused now, but it will come again soon. Earlier this evening, I walked to our two-track driveway and up to the road where I can get cell reception. I called my lover. She is spending the night with my mother down in the Twin Cities, as she had a training for work to attend there. Tomorrow she plans to make the five hour drive here to visit. That means tomorrow I must prepare for her. This consists of cleaning out the tent, cutting fresh firewood, and picking a bouquet of wildflowers.

When we spoke on the phone, she told me she had made arrangements for our wedding, which will occur in less than two months. We will have a small wedding by the lake in Bemidji, with a Justice of the Peace performing the ceremony. We are inviting fewer than ten people, mostly because I have a difficult time expressing sentiments in a crowd, and I want to be able to express them to her on that day. After the rituals, we will guide the participants here to camp and spend the night.

It's strange to consider the idea of getting married without either of our parents present. Not that I had any preconceived notion of a large grandiose wedding. In fact, I prefer it to happen in privacy so that I may say what I feel without editing my words for other people's ears. None of our family or friends know of our wedding date. I hope they are pleased with the surprise, but I really don't care either way.

As I previously mentioned, today I began to write. I started off the day by finishing my read of *Canoeing with the Cree*. It was splendid and amazing and I wanted to live that adventure. I then began to work on my own writing. Unfortunately, the 12volt deep-cycle gel battery I had hooked up to my solar power system was not sufficient enough to power my laptop for very long. I walked to the Jeep and carried the eighty-pound commercial grade battery to camp.

I placed the battery on a box above ground in the small tent that houses the rest of my solar electronics.

I then ran a parallel wiring from the charge controller to the smaller battery, then to this larger one, and from there to the power inverter. I plugged in the extension cord and hooked up my laptop. The power supply was perfect for the rest of the day, never dropping below 12.3 volts. Before coming to bed, realizing it would rain, I disconnected all power cables from the batteries and shut everything down. I did not install a grounding rod because with all the tall trees around, lightning will naturally be attracted to one of them, and a grounding rod would only invite a lightning strike closer to my tent. So, whenever there is a potential for a storm, I will unplug everything. This adds to the list of daily chores to remember, but I am still well below the requirements of a more civilized life.

I plan to get to bed earlier tonight, not only to avoid the cold, but also so I may awake sooner tomorrow than I did today. I hope to get several good hours of writing in before preparing camp for Mayana's visit. After that, I would like to wander to the riffle in the river and try my luck wading with a fly rod, casting for muskie. The summer is half over and I've barely spent time in this pursuit. Ten-thousand casts is a long ways to go.

July 29 Friday

I have slept at camp approximately fifty nights. The only way I know the date is by looking at the header of the previous day's journal entry. I am only aware that today is Friday because today my woman arrives.

This morning I awoke with blood on my feet, so I promptly washed and bandaged them so not to get infected. Over a month camping alone in the wild without a wound. I must admit, that is a great safety record, considering everything that could go wrong out here.

Last night I had the most horrific dream. I was tied flat on a board, legs and arms bound, and placed here in this forest. I was not afraid of bears or wolves licking their lips and eating me alive. There was an image much worse than being picked apart by ravens and turkey vultures, or being slowly devoured by ants and beetles. I was being attacked, engulfed in a flying flame of mosquitoes. I flailed about helplessly as they quickly began to devour my blood. There were thousands of them. They clouded out the entire visible world. Finally, I broke my hands free and began swatting the air furiously, but it was hopeless. They clung to my skin. I screamed in my loudest, deepest voice. It was my death cry, one last verbal effort to fight them off. Then I awoke with sweat on my brow, slapping my hands all over my body. I didn't want to go back to sleep, but I couldn't step outside because I could hear the real-life swarms waiting for me. Finally, I shut my eyes to slumber again. This time I dreamt of the ancient Native Americans and wondered what tactics they developed to survive these ferocious beasts.

When I awoke this morning, I found the bloody claw marks on my feet. At first I thought I had been acting out my dream, but upon closer inspection, I realized there were actual bites all over my feet. Several mosquitoes had been trapped in my tent all night, feasting on my exposed feet. I will do a mosquito check in the tent every night before going to bed.

I took my first shower of the week this morning. I figured since my lover is coming, I should get clean. There are more mosquitoes in the forest than trees, and there are a lot of trees. Just as I filled the shower pail, it began to rain. I decided to postpone the shower while I emptied and cleaned the rain buckets that have been sitting full since the last rain several nights ago. After they were cleaned and placed at their locations, I stood beneath a spout of rain that came down off the awning and washed my hair. It didn't rain for long, each bucket is now one-third full, but it looks as though it will rain sporadically throughout the day.

Now I will walk up to the road for cell reception and call Mayana. If she is coming tonight, I will return and take a full shower. If she isn't coming until tomorrow, I will wait until morning.

...

It's now evening. I had a shower earlier. It may have been the most unpleasant experience of my life.

The mosquito netting I had draped over the bucket was intended to act as a barrier and protect me from these repulsive beasts, but it clung to my wet and naked flesh. This allowed them to attack me while I stood crouched down beneath a dirty old sock that was spurting out cold rainwater. I lit two citronella candles nearby, thinking they would repel these blood thirsty predators, but the vapors burned my eyes so intensely that I was temporarily blinded. Mosquitoes are drawn to two things: water and heat. I presented an easy access to both. I felt like I was entombed in Saran wrap that was laced with tiny needles and had a poisonous fog in constant circulation. I wondered what the hell I was thinking with this insidious contraption. I was inspired to bathe quickly.

...

I spent several hours writing my novel today. While I have hopeful expectations of its success, I also wonder if I will be able to write it the way it deserves. It reads witty and poetic to me, but will others be frustrated and close the book after page five, wishing they had spent their money on something more productive, such as pizza delivery.

Pizza. I haven't craved it since I've been here. In fact, the only things I have craved are walks to the river, reading in tranquility with only the sounds of birds and a breeze, and the sight of wildlife. Everything but the last has happened as easily as ordering a pizza would in town. The wildlife have mostly eluded me. I have seen the signs of animals. On a walk to the river earlier today, I saw a track that was either a badger or raccoon; difficult to tell the way the mud had engulfed it. The last two nights I have heard the howl of wolves and the hooting of owls. So they are around, but they haven't gotten the courage to introduce themselves yet.

My woman will be here any minute. I'm going to straighten up camp and try to look presentable. We're going to have some fun tonight.

July 30 Saturday

I am less productive while Mayana is here, and that is alright. We slept in late, woke up for something to eat, and then returned to a long nap until mid-afternoon. Shortly after we arose, it began to rain. I hoped it would sustain, for my rain barrels are nearly empty, but it lasted only thirty minutes. It's a muggy day so it will rain again soon.

After the rain cleared, we took an exploratory journey in the Jeep. I was hesitant to leave camp, because I have been here over six weeks without leaving, but I decided it was time for a brief vacation. We haven't seen much of the area surrounding our land, so we drove and stopped at five lakes within a ten-mile radius. They were all unique and majestic. Our favorite was Erskine Lake, a little pothole lake of thirty-nine acres. Its shoreline was beautiful with hills of pine trees descending down to the crystalline water. The best part was that the lake has rainbow trout. I felt a subliminal pull in my casting arm from the proximity of these fish.

...

We are back at camp now, and Mayana started a fire to prepare dinner. It's great having somebody take some of the daily chores, and I must admit, I enjoy the passion she displays while doing them. Conversely, having the extra person here creates more chores for me and adds a sense of urgency to everything. She tells me this is my camp more than hers, which I understand since I am constantly telling her where something is or where something goes. But it is her camp as much as mine. Dinner is ready. If the weather holds, we may go for a moonlit canoe ride.

July 31 Sunday

It rained good and long last night. Been waiting for it all week, watching my water supply dry up. It's pouring now as we sit outside the tent under the canopy. We bathed ourselves in the rain as it spurted off the canvas roof. This reminded me of something only a child would do. It's a good storm, with lots of thunder and lightning, but little wind. All the rain buckets got full in twenty minutes—that will last the rest of the week.

...

We took a canoe ride up the river after the storm, and left the dogs secured at camp. It's the farthest I've gone up the river so far. It truly is a remote wilderness, and we felt as though our paddles were the only ones to have touched the river in many years. Approximately two miles upstream, we came upon our first evidence of mankind, a large old farmhouse settlement. This was where we turned around and began to fish. We used spinning rods, hoping to catch something for dinner. Mayana caught the first fish from our river, a good-size walleye that she hooked in a grassy shallow using a jighead and worm we had dug up near camp. It tasted delicious when we fried it over the fire.

Mayana decided to stay the night, meaning she'll leave at 5:30 a.m. tomorrow for work. It's been great having her company here, listening to all of her wandering thoughts. I am continually amazed at the shape of her mind. I do get frustrated at times with little things that would go unnoticed living in a house, but here in the woods mean much more, such as forgetting to put the cap on something, leaving a bag of chips lying out, or sleeping on the bed while wearing dirty clothes. I'm sure after spending more time here, she'll learn to appreciate these things.

I'm going to make this entry short so that we can spend the rest of her time here together. Tomorrow I begin another week alone.

August 1 Monday

Everything seems louder here while alone. I walked Mayana to her car this morning at 5:15, and I've been awake since. I finished reading *Lord Jim*. It was a manly and courageous story with an honorable ending. The reading was mostly dull, except for a few memorable quotes. It was constantly changing narratives, and I often forgot who was telling the story.

Sly has been acting cautious all day, stopping for long smells where he usually runs past, then looking up at me quizzically, either trying to tell me what he smells or wondering if I know what it is. I've felt the presence of a bear. Sly too has felt something. He often comes out of his tent and walks halfway to the edge of camp where he lowers his head and stares intently. I call him back to prevent an affront.

I do not fear the bear. I keep my knife on my belt and my camera close, ready for either of the two encounters that could happen. I have concealed the food at camp as much as possible. I will start a fire soon and put smoke in the air to disguise any residual scents. There's a lot of noise in the forest tonight. Lots of branches breaking.

I built a small bookshelf for the tent today. I used two small pine trees with trunks approximately three inches in diameter, and assembled the pieces using twine. It turned out well; the books rest level, and it's not so bad to look at.

The deerflies have become a nuisance, but if I compare them to the horseflies, they don't seem so bad. Horseflies can get up to one and one-quarter inches long, and they buzz erratically around my head in loud mechanical vibrations. Only the females eat flesh—the males are nectavores—so I don't get bitten that often. But when I do, I know it, and there will be a large welt to remind me later. While the horseflies attack at random locations on my body, these deerflies primarily go for the head.

A fire would seem more inviting if Mayana were here to share it, so I will sit in the darkness alone. I do love my solitude. I don't have to consider anyone else's wants; I start a fire when I choose. There's no one to divide chores with, and even though that may sound easier, I generally prefer to do them myself rather than explain what needs to be done.

When I called Mayana earlier this evening, she

told me there is a seven-state heat advisory warning, including Minnesota. So I shouldn't expect to sweat any less, or for my ice to last very long. Now I will start a fire, and say damn the heat. The flames will be my company.

The fire is burning well. I put the remainder of the chicken, wrapped in tinfoil, into the fire. This will be Sly's treat for the rest of the week. I brought the garbage up to the Jeep; it was getting quite rank. I will send it back with Mayana after her next visit.

When Mayana is here, I often hope a bear will enter camp so that I may show a display of barbaric manliness by protecting her. When she is away, the last thing I want to see in camp is a bear. A sighting anywhere else would be welcomed, but here, alone, I mostly worry about a bear coming into camp while I am asleep and tearing into my supplies.

Maybe I could befriend the bear, make a neighbor of him. How does one go about doing something like that? I can't offer him a plate of fresh-caught walleye as a welcome-to-the-neighborhood gift; mostly because I haven't caught any walleye, but also because he would undoubtedly want more. I don't imagine a bear would become as domesticated through handouts as a dog, and though it's uncommon, it's not unheard of for a black bear to attack a person. More people are killed by black bears than grizzlies, though I suspect that is due to the fact there are more of them, and more people frequent black bear country than grizzly country. I believe I could fight one off with my armory of bladed weapons if I had to, but these beasts get quite large in the north, so it would be a good fight.

A lot of ranting about the bears when, actually, I'm not concerned. Worst-case scenario — death by a bear while living freely in my forest—sounds better than any of the thousand deaths that could kill me in the city. Getting dark now; time to let the fire hypnotize me into that world of sleep.

...

I have decided the mosquitoes don't care if it's going to rain, if it's raining, or has recently rained. They don't care if it's sunny or cloudy, calm or windy. They don't care if it's morning, afternoon, evening, or night. They don't care if I'm wearing pants or shorts, T-shirt or long sleeves. All they want is my blood. They want to devour me until I am a pile of bones. They cause more mental horror than physical pain. They enjoy me most when I am at the latrine, so I make my visits there as brief as possible, keeping as much skin covered as I can. They attack my eyes and fingertips, suckle from my nose, and bite through my socks. They attack me from below until I start slapping myself as a jockey would his horse while racing in a derby. I run back to my tent as quickly as I can, thinking I may never step outside again.

I no longer believe that a bear, or any other animal, could survive in these woods. The mosquitoes would devour them. They must all live underground. I imagine elaborate underground labyrinths where all the animals congregate in a treaty of peace and coexistence to avoid the mosquitoes. The animal tracks I have seen around camp were made by crepuscular clones. These clones were designed to fetch food and return it to the underground chambers. The clones spend time aboveground, and so are familiar with the mosquitoes, which has caused them to become mosquito crazy. I have contracted the disease.

I cleaned my ears using a Q-tip for the first time since

my arrival. I assumed there would be massive wads of orange and yellow slimy goo. This was not the case. The Q-tip came out barely tinted. Perhaps earwax is a self-defense mechanism developed by the white noise of city life. It's designed to help mute out all the unwanted noises coming from machines and electricity and other people's voices. In the forest, I require my audio reception to be clear, perfect, untainted. I am constantly perking my ears to register minute sounds a couple hundred feet away. In the city, I would never hear the hopping of a frog, even if I were standing directly above it, looking down.

Another audio phenomenon I have realized is that, during the day, I cannot hear the river riffle a mile away. This in itself is no surprise, considering the density of the forest between camp and the water. However, about two hours after dark, I begin to hear the riffle as clearly as though I were standing in the middle of a mountain stream. Why is this? The trees are still there. The river doesn't turn up the volume after dark. I believe it is Solar Distortion.

I am not certain if Solar Distortion is an actual term in the realm of scientific nomenclature, but if it isn't, it should be. It seems most evident to me, being here and listening to the natural world for twenty-four hours a day, that the sun has a subliminal voice. It speaks to all living things underneath the ambient sounds, behind their conscious perceptions, so that they never actually recognize hearing it. But it is there. When the sun retreats for the evening, the invisible photons which were filling the air continue to bounce around for a couple hours until they lose their energy and fade away. Now the sun is no longer heard. All these other faint noises that I don't hear during daylight become loud and noticeable. The sunbeams fill up the empty spaces between the trees and deflect the sounds of the river. At night, there is no Solar Distortion, so the sound of the river travels farther. After dark, among the songs of a river riffle, I feel to be back in the mountains with the music of a trout stream rushing around me.

...

I wrote 3,200 words in my novel today. In my spare time I have been reading *Look Homeward, Angel* by Thomas Wolfe. In the introduction written by his editor and friend Max Perkins, it is mentioned that Tom was once heard walking down a European street at night singing, "I wrote ten-thousand words today!" I've got a long way to go. Getting a third of the way there on a rainy day when I was unable to use my laptop for most of it due to reduced solar charge is a good start. I am certain that on the right day, with the right focus, I can achieve that goal. But only if the ten-thousand words are worth writing.

Another week at camp complete. I will get seven to nine more, depending on the weather and my tenacity. Remaining clean and organized is the key to success here. Now I will make a light vodka drink to guide me to bed.

August 2 Tuesday

The wind howls fiercely tonight. I remember cursing the wind when I lived in Casper, Wyoming. It was the force that drove me to insanity. So it's ironic that when the wind blows here it drives away the local force of my insanity. It has been the mildest day for mosquitoes so far. Here the wind is the proprietor of my sanity. Though the paradox is that my sanity put a crazy smile on my face. I walked around camp bare-chested most of the day, which was great because it was extremely hot. No other day have I been able to stand outside fully clothed for more than thirty seconds without cursing the skies that give mosquitoes flight. I still slapped the occasional one from my skin, but it was so infrequent that this act only served as a reminder of my previous days' torment. I was even able to go down to the hammock by the river for an early evening nap.

On my walk towards the river, I spotted bear tracks in the fresh mud from yesterday's rain. Must have passed through last night or early morning. These tracks were smaller than the ones I had noticed a week ago, though they passed on the same section of my trail. I am left to assume that a sow and cub make that walk regularly, and only after a rain do I see their tracks. How convenient for me that they cross my trail at its muddiest location, so I know they were here. One of these days I shall sleep all day so that I can stay up all night and watch for them.

I wrote 2,100 words today. Not as productive as yesterday, but these were some of my best. I need to write my best in higher numbers if I am going to fill a novel. For this I require sunny days. It was cloudy for the middle-half of today and rained for thirty minutes. This makes it difficult to keep my laptop charged. I leave the solar panel on unless there's lightning present, in which case I unplug everything.

When it is sunny and the solar power system is active, I wait until my laptop battery drops to 50 percent, then plug it in to let it charge; this allows the deep-cycle batteries to acquire a charge from the solar panels in between uses. I am constantly getting up to check the voltage. If it gets below 11.9 volts, I turn off the inverter and let the panels charge the battery to at least 12.2 volts. While this is happening, I cannot charge my laptop, and the battery only lasts about two hours. All of this creates delay and distraction from my writing, but I think I am much more creative out here alone than trying to write in town with unlimited electrical supply and infinite distractions.

The wind is causing my tent walls to pulsate. Sly smells of rotten fish. My lamp light is fading. The vodka drink is getting low.

August 3 Wednesday
Every day I wake up alone with a river. Every day I

am the first and only human to see this shoreline. Every morning, afternoon, and evening I am the only human who knows these trees. All day long, I am the sole representative of the human species in this forest. This is a great opportunity and an enormous responsibility, and I do it well.

There's a place where the trail descends down a hill to the river. At the right time of morning, the sunlight shines directly through a small clearing in the trees and looks like a spotlight illuminating the forest floor. Where the sun touches the soil and plants and decaying wood, every miniscule life form becomes active. There are insects of colors no paintbrush could replicate, designed so small and versatile that no mind of man could create. In the shade surrounding this small stage, nothing moves—at least not visibly—but in this light there is life in abundance. As the sun slowly travels across the trail, I see new life forms presented, and they take full advantage of what little time they have in this warmth. When the sun passes and the shade returns, they disappear back into the hidden world from which they came. I watch the cycle until the sun has been blocked by the trees, and then I return to the river.

On the shore there is a decaying log set perpendicular to the river, and I sit to look upstream at the water flowing towards me. The water is different every second, and I cannot help but be amazed by the mosaic of colors. The trees and the landscape converge on the surface of the river and blend in abstract variations. If I were a better man, I would be a painter. What a great feeling it must be to recreate something as beautiful as this, but to make it my own. The best I can do is write it. Perhaps I will design the protagonist of my novel as a painter. If the imagination does not take what is real and make it better, then it has lost its purpose.

August 4 Thursday

I am tired tonight. This is a good thing because it implies I am growing comfortable. Every other night, I've sat up with a drink, reading myself to sleep. Tomorrow Mayana arrives. That means tomorrow is Friday. Time moves incredibly slowly out here. It's been a productive week, full of physical lethargy and mental exuberance. I added ten-thousand words to my story in four days. If I can do that every week for six more weeks, I will have a full-length novel. Most novels fall into the range of fifty to one-hundred thousand words.

It is already getting dark. I don't know what time it is, but it certainly is earlier than a week ago for this same degree of sunlight. During all the years of living in a house with the clocks and routines, I never noticed the difference of daylight in a single week. Here the sun is my only light. I have a lamp that's bright enough to write this journal or, with squinty eyes, read a book held up to my face, but I still notice the absence of sunlight more; I am more affected by it. I know when I hear the frog hop onto the tarp outside my tent, the sun has officially set. I know darkness when I can no longer see the white bark of aspen trees only fifteen feet away.

...

There have been a lot of new spiders active these past few days. There is one species, which is particularly interesting, whose large webs I've noticed in abundance. I've made the mistake of walking into a few. Now every time I walk the trail, I wave a stick up and down in front of me. These spiders are the size of the top half of my thumb. They have long eyes and a furry back. Their abdomen is yellow, and their legs are black with yellow stripes.

There are numerous animal sounds surrounding my tent tonight. I will get my camera ready with the flash, turn out the lamp, and sit by the screen window, waiting for one to sound in range. This is far more interesting than any television station.

August 5 Friday

It's been a good time so far, and I could live here forever. Of course, I'd have to improvise my camp for the deep cold of winter. But then my meat would stay fresh, and my beer would always be cold. Last night was my first night at camp without an alcoholic beverage. I don't drink to get drunk, but mostly as an aid to help me ignore the chill of nocturnal air and the mosquitoes who dominate the night.

I'm making this entry earlier than most days. It's now mid-evening and Mayana should have already left Bemidji. She mentioned earlier this week that we could meet at the tavern in Effie. I've been thinking about a frothy beer poured cold from the tap ever since she suggested it. I haven't seen another person in many weeks. I should have missed people-watching by now, and be anxious for that opportunity, but the truth is I haven't even thought about it. I've seen so many people in my life, and they all still exist in my mind.

Earlier today, in the name of muscular exercise, I decided to finish the wooden walkway section of our path. There is a segment of trail near the driveway that is lower grade and collects water every time it rains. I wanted to build a boardwalk so we didn't bring extra mud into camp. To accomplish this, I used a carpentry saw and axe. I found fallen trees from the forest, only using fresher ones that hadn't begun to rot. I selected sections that were between two and four inches in diameter, and then cut lengths of approximately twenty inches and lay them side-by-side, perpendicular to the trail. The boardwalk spans fifty feet of trail. This took an incredible number of pieces, figuring the average length of trail being covered by each piece was three inches. That's approximately two-hundred cuts with my handsaw. I worked my forearms, had a good sweat, and the trail looks great. Now I need a good rain so I can stomp them into the mud and secure them in place.

The deerflies outnumbered the mosquitoes today, but now there are also these tiny "no-see-ums" present in great numbers. They are annoying, but I prefer either of these insects over the swarms of mosquitoes. I still get the not-so-friendly reminder of the mosquito whenever I stand outside, and it is often their high-pitched scream that bothers me more than the bite.

I cleaned out the tent today to prepare for my conjugal visit. I found three big, fat, white ticks that must have fallen from Sly. I've been giving him a quick check every night, but I must now be more thorough.

If someone ever wanted to make a scary movie about

wood ticks, there would be no exaggeration necessary. If you have ever seen an army of them running up your pant legs, if you have ever removed your lover's shirt to find a multitude attached to her back, if you have ever seen the ceiling of your tent littered with them on a starry night, then you know of their horror. They are grotesque and gluttonous little bastards. Their flat bodies can go unnoticed wherever they decide to infiltrate your skin. That is, until they have eaten so much of you they become grossly fat, white globules the size of a thumbnail. They can increase their body weight ten-fold within a couple of days. Once they are full, they will lay their eggs and then drop to live off their fat until the next victim comes along. I feel lucky that I can count on both hands and feet the number I have pulled from my skin, and most of them had not snuck their little flesh-eating heads into me.

It was late afternoon when I began to work on my novel. I wasn't focused today, but still managed to whip out 1,800 words. Nothing too substantial or insightful, but it got the plot moving. A little fluff is necessary to carry every novel.

Mayana will be here soon. I'm going to cut some firewood and get it burning. I will deny her request for a visit to the Effie Tavern tonight; I'm not ready to leave camp quite yet.

Quick amendment: the mosquitoes still exist in swarms at the latrine. They wait for me where I am most vulnerable and defenseless. They are remarkable strategists!

August 6 Saturday

Today was a grand day. We woke up early to the sounds of wind and rain. Fell back into a deep sleep and stayed there until late morning. Woke up and had a home cooked breakfast compliments of Mayana's wilderness kitchen. Went back to the tent and I read while Mayana napped. Emerged from the tent for camp mochas (instant hot chocolate packets added to instant coffee) and conversation. Ate a few tacos. Had another bag of fresh cookies that Mayana baked at home. Admired Mayana's bounty of weekly provisions. Went for a long walk encompassing about two-thirds of the property's perimeter. Bushwhacked through parts we hadn't seen before.

We identified several species of flowering plants new to us, our favorite being the spotted touch-me-not. We also discovered a grove of elm trees whose short vertical branches created a bright forest floor and a better view than the tangled mesh of fir trees around camp. Perhaps this is where we will build a cabin someday. It would be nice to have our cabin on a separate half of the property and keep this place reserved for more primitive camping.

We came out through the unmarked forest at the animal trail that parallels the river. We followed this down into the creek valley that cuts through our property west to east and enters the river. All along the edges were fresh deer tracks. During our walk, we heard the high-pitched, screaming whistle of bald eagles, and shortly after returning to camp, we saw one soaring above us. This is the second eagle I have seen here; the other was soaring above us as we paddled the canoe downstream towards the rapids another day. I anticipated seeing them more frequently, considering this river boasts the highest population of breeding bald eagles in the contiguous U.S.

We then started a fire. Mayana enjoys this task and

is quite good at it, so when she is here I let her handle that pleasure. It has been a chilly day, with barely a sight of the sun, which was displeasing because I had hoped to charge up my solar batteries while not in use. I haven't done any writing in my novel while she has been at camp.

August 7 Sunday

A light drizzle just began. I heard the sounds of a large animal rush through the forest about one-hundred feet away. The sky light is fading. I will let the rain extinguish the small fire.

It's been a rather eventful day. Canyon got his first swimming lesson and first canoe ride. I tried casting flies while wading off our shoreline. That was difficult because Sly was in a swimming frenzy. He swam in circles around me, and whenever I tried to make a cast, he thought the splash of my fly was made by a fish, and he paddled himself over to check it out. It was all I could do to keep my hook out of him. This continued for over thirty minutes, Sly not putting his feet on solid ground the entire time. He is a swimming, fishing fool. We have a lot in common. I didn't catch a thing. Even after Mayana and Canyon returned from their canoe ride, and she offered to bring Sly up to camp, still nothing.

After a hot dinner of delicious pasta and spiced hamburger, we took a naturalist excursion through the forest. Mayana carried her camera and I the identification guides. This forest is filled with great diversity of species. I focused primarily on those in flower or fruit. I can now identify half a dozen new specimens. We found a raspberry bramble and picked some of their soft, furry, succulent fruits for instant consumption.

While up at the driveway, we met our neighbor, who introduced himself as Indian Joe. He owns a vacant forty acre plot adjacent to ours. He seems to be a compassionate and taciturn woodsman. He told me of the northern pike he had caught from the river, and the bull moose he saw this morning.

Mayana and I returned to camp and I started a small fire while she gave me a slideshow presentation of her weekend photos. Some things look more beautiful captured on camera, but they lack the vividness of living exposure.

It's getting dark. She's already in the tent. The rain has stopped. I should join her.

I am disappointed with my solar power setup. I charged all the batteries earlier during this sunny day, only drawing power to charge my cell phone for thirty minutes. The battery voltage never got above 11.8. I like to see it above 12.0. It's going to be difficult to charge my laptop. I may have to pack the battery out next week and bring it someplace where I can give it a full, deep charge.

August 8 Monday

The mosquitoes are fierce tonight, but they are not my concern. All day I heard the deep growling *moo* of bears. They started their calls middle of last night in between camp and the river. Today, out of curiosity, I referenced my mammal guidebook and learned this is their mating season. This evening, as I sit outside writing, I hear their calls in several directions. They sound less than two-hundred feet away. I'm glad that earlier today, in preparation for my first trip back to town tomorrow, I fully scent-proofed my camp. Included in this task was taking my urine bottle from the tent and splashing generous amounts at all camp entrances. I now sit beside a small fire hoping the smoke will cover any lingering aromas.

I just heard a series of loud knocking sounds coming from the creek valley less than a hundred feet away. My only concern is a territorial male coming into camp. I will not fear them, simply because I cannot. If I start to fear them, I do not belong in these woods. Though, in fairness, the rabbit fears the bear and this is still his home. I just heard a wolf howl, and there are owls hooting in the distance. This truly is a wild kingdom.

Several times while writing this page I have stood up and considered going into my tent. But I persevere. Here I remain. I have already put Sly inside, for his curious ears and glances into the forest make me worry about him running off into the darkness and confronting a bear. I imagine the bear would be afraid, since Sly looks wolfish, and wolves attack bears. Black bears can get pretty big around here, easily twice my weight or five of Sly's. That's a lot of beast wrapped up in one package.

...

I am now inside the tent. I look out the window and watch the embers of my fire fade to white. I generally don't leave an unattended fire, but tonight I want as much smoke wafting into the air as possible. I lit a citronella candle outside my tent to disguise any edible scents. I'm not sure if the splashing of my urine at camp entrances was a good thing, or if it would cause aggression in a territorial male bear. I hear the occasional mooing growl in the proximal forest. I just heard the hard knocking of a tree near the creek. Part of me wishes I had a pistol. Instead, I have a hunting knife on one side of my belt and a KA-BAR machete on the other. This is the loudest a night has been since my arrival.

That's enough talk of bears, though I just heard one snort. It is blackness outside all of the windows. If they come, they come. I'm ready. There's nothing else I can do to prevent it. What does the bear think of this world where his ancestors roamed freely but is now surrounded by areas ruled by men?

So, new topic for distraction. I tied a beautiful fly today. It resembles the shape, size, color, and movement of the baitfish I have seen in the river. I hope to arise early and fish tomorrow before driving to town. Driving to town. I don't like the sound of that. Especially now with all the wildlife present and active. I enjoy the mystery and the constant edge of fear. Plus, I should be here to guard camp. A lot could happen during two days in town. I've decided to go back midweek because Mayana wants to go to the Effie rodeo this weekend, which means we will stay here during that time. That's going to be a lot of proximity to people in the next few days.

My primary reason for leaving tomorrow is because of my solar power system; it simply won't get charged above 11.8 volts. I need at least 12.0 to be comfortable charging my laptop enough to write. Today I sat in my Jeep with the engine running for two hours while charging my laptop using an inverter plugged into the cigarette lighter outlet. This is not only a dilemma, but also a distraction. The problem initiated when I ran my laptop on a cloudy and rainy day.

The river sounds like a highway tonight, and I want to ride it. This is my home; not inside these canvas walls, but inside the spaces between the trees. My home is also with Mayana; she holds my heart while the forest holds my soul. These are my two loves, the forces I live to impress. I am ruled by neither but loyal to both. I am a lucky man, for I have two loves who get along with each other.

The forest displays a subtle love. It is in the way she reciprocates my silence while also singing me sweet songs. It is in the way she touches me gently as I pass through her. It is in the way she hides me from the world and asks no questions. I have a need and a value for both of my loves. I am treated with appreciation by both of my loves. I am a lucky man; I am a man with two hearts.

It is time to put down the pencil and read. It's getting late. I may not rise in time to fish. But I must fish, for if I do not catch a fish from this river during my stay here, I will regret it all winter. Though regret can develop an unrivaled power in men. If applied correctly, regret can influence you to chase a goal with greater ambition.

In the morning, I fish.

August 9 Tuesday

It is early morning and I just returned from the river without a catch. I wanted to bring home fresh fillets so I could taste the wilderness while being in the city. Now I must leave and drive to town. I will see you soon, dear forest friend of mine.

August 10 Wednesday

Not knowing what to do with myself here in town, I spent most of the afternoon on the back porch watching the birds. In the forest, I hear many birds but rarely see them. I tried to identify through the sight of birds in our yard the songs of those in the wild, but they sing a different song here; those hidden songs of the forest canopy are much more beautiful. I believe we all sing our best while in the freedom of the trees.

After the neighbor came out and started running his loud, smoking lawn mower, I went inside and paced around. I spent much time looking through our bookshelves and discovered three titles that had something in common. These three books each had a section written about the river beside my camp. The books were: *The Streams and Rivers of Minnesota*, written by Thomas F. Waters and published by the University of MN Press; *America's Wild and Scenic Rivers*, by the National Geographic Society; and *Wild Rivers of North America*, by Michael Jenkinson. Here's an excerpt from Waters: the river has areas… "with unsurpassed wilderness qualities."

This river corridor was home to Native Americans for at least two-thousand years. In the 1880's, European settlers began using the river as a logging highway, cutting down trees from the nearby forest and sending them downstream, north towards the Canadian border. There are still places where you can find stumps larger than four feet in diameter — remnants of an indigenous forest more wild than today's. The river is 165 miles long, and even now it is encompassed mostly by wilderness, only passing through two small towns during its route to a confluence with the Rainy River, which separates the U.S. from Canada.

While it was the loggers who ultimately settled the land, it was the fur trade that first drew settlers to this area of the Northwoods. These men were known as Voyageurs, and the rivers were their life-blood and where they drew their sustenance, which was mostly derived from trapping beaver. More recently, in 1963, this river was one of four to be inducted into a new *Minnesota State Water Trails System*. This system was implemented to help protect some of the most scenic and pristine waterways in the state. I was happy to read about the river and acquire a deeper appreciation for its history, but this made me want to be there and never return to a house or city.

When Mayana came home, we went to dinner at a local pizzeria. It was strange sitting in there, a room compacted with strangers and so much noise. I missed our dinners in the sanctuary of the forest. But the pizza was delicious.

Mayana has gone off to bed as I sit outside alone, finishing a beer and updating this journal. A plane flew over and I heard the neighborhood dogs barking at it. I wonder if the wolves are howling tonight. I wonder if bears have destroyed my camp. I wonder if vermin have made a nest out of my books in the tent.

August 11 Thursday

I have arrived at camp. On my drive here, I felt hesitant. During my two days in a house, I had acclimated to the city life. I had forgotten what a luxury it was to turn on a sink or open the refrigerator. I enjoyed going out to dinner and having somebody else do the cooking. None of those luxuries are available in the woods, and for the entire drive, I thought they would be missed. I thought I was making a mistake living as the rugged recluse.

The moment I stepped out of the Jeep, I was attacked by deer flies and mosquitoes. I opened up the passenger door and the crate with my water jugs fell to the ground, causing one third of this week's supply to spill out. By this point I was sweating profusely in the humid air. I carried my first eighty pound load to camp, and twisted my ankle in a rabbit hole.

I entered the clearing and saw the sun reflecting off my canvas tent. There were new flowers blooming along the trail, and a fisher scurried under the ferns. I heard the screeching of an eagle and the rustling of aspen leaves in the ow sky. These sights and sounds performed as a sedative would within me, and I felt entirely calm.

I have kept my clothes in a large waterproof pack outside the tent. I opened it to put in clean laundry and, upon doing so, noticed a mouse had chewed a hole in the side. I held it upright and shook out all the contents. A large mouse plopped onto the floor and scurried under the tent platform, stunned from the fall. As I shook off my clothes to rid them of any mouse scat, I noticed a small pink slimy baby mouse on the ground. I picked it up and placed it by the platform where its mother took shelter. As I shuffled though the clothes, I found five more, a total of six baby mice. I placed the rest with the first and built a small nest over top so they wouldn't be discovered by the dogs. I don't know if the mother will take them back, but if she does, I will have added six more rodents to my camp that will inevitably get back into my supplies. So why did I attempt to save them instead of scattering them into the woods? I don't know the answer, except it seemed right. I believe that every creature given a chance at life should get a chance to live it. Well, maybe not the mosquito.

I took a walk to the river, taking time to notice the changes since my departure. Wild sarsaparilla has come into fruit. I noticed other plants flowering that I haven't yet identified. Then I came to the only muddy section of trail, which runs ten feet before dropping to the river. Here was a cub-sized bear track, multiple deer tracks of various sizes, and one wolf track. There must be many wild creatures roaming these woods if this many leave tracks at a single location.

August 12 Friday

Sly made the most unusual and annoying sound today while he was locked at camp and I was in the river fishing. I was half a mile away but could hear his screams clearly. He sounded like a calf being eaten alive by a coyote; and yes, that is something I have heard.

It happened early one morning in east central Wyoming, in the Powder River basin. I had arrived at a ranch in the middle of nowhere to measure river flow and collect water samples from the creek that flowed through the property. I was walking through a field of sagebrush, watching the sun crest over the distant prairie, when I heard a horrific squeal coming from the other side of a hill. I remember this distinctly because I almost stepped on a rattlesnake that was still coiled up to retain warmth from a cool night. I diverted my route to investigate. When I came to the top of the hill, I saw a small drinking hole where the cattle went for their morning sip, but the cattle who were there seemed uninterested in the water and were more concerned with what was happening nearby. To the west of the pond, I saw a coyote with its face buried in the abdomen of a young calf. The calf was still alive and was making the most horrific sound I ever heard. The coyote occasionally looked up at the other cows circling nearby. Its face was covered in blood and guts, and it looked happy. It didn't take long before the life left the calf and the morning returned to silence, but I can still remember that sound clearly, and it is almost the exact noise Sly made while he was locked in the tent this morning.

I couldn't concentrate on fishing for long with that sound ringing down the river corridor, so I returned to camp without a catch and freed him from the tent. He came out and took a few steps before lying down. This upset me because he could have easily lay in his tent where there were no mosquitoes and let me fish. Oh well, now I will spend the rest of the day writing. There will be time to fish again. There is always time to fish in Minnesota.

August 13 Saturday
Early this morning, Mayana woke me to the sound of a bear grunting through our woods. We lay awake and listened to it for a while; it seemed to be following the creek near camp towards the river. Shortly after, I heard a large varmint shuffle across the tent platform. We fell back asleep, and when I finally arose several hours later, I checked on the baby mice that I had removed a couple days ago; they were gone. My suspicion is that the mother came and snatched them away during the night, for the

shelter I had built was undisturbed, and only a mouse could be small enough to enter it without disruption.

This weekend is the Effie rodeo, the only time of year when the population of Effie (a small village 8 miles west of camp) rises above one-hundred people. All day we heard motorcycles and cars in the distance, along with somebody nearby firing off their rifle, most likely sighting it in for hunting season. All of these sounds annoy me. I am here for silence. Even though it is just one weekend, part of me wanted to assassinate the man with the rifle.

We voyaged into town to check out the rodeo. It's certainly the most cowboys I've seen since leaving Wyoming. We arrived too late, and the events had just finished, so we rode on and stopped at the tavern for a couple of beers. Not much doing there; we played the jukebox, finished our drinks, then left. There will be more events tomorrow.

We arrived back at camp and promptly prepared dinner. Soon we will go down to the river and have a fire in the rock ring I made earlier today.

Last night I heard a single wolf howl as I sat by the fire after Mayana had retired to bed. Earlier today, I started reading *Robinson Crusoe*. I had gotten tired of the slow pace in *Look Homeward, Angel*, even though it's a poetic style of prose. I will continue it someday. I have started and stopped *Robinson Crusoe* several times, this time I will finish it. I need to start writing again. It has been almost a week since I worked on my novel. My thoughts have been filled with new ideas. Monday I will immerse myself in them.

The mosquitoes have been mild today. Earlier I prepared a shower for Mayana, and the citronella candle that I normally place beside wasn't necessary.

We heard loons flying over camp today, and also the screeching of a bald eagle. It rained lightly this morning while we were lying in bed, but not enough to make it worth getting up to refill the rain barrels.

I sit by the river making this entry while Mayana is at camp preparing dinner. I have no list of chores and no television to resign my thoughts to. This is a great life.

August 14 Sunday

Last night we made a fire by the river beside an old-growth cedar (after a few beers, we named that tree Bartholomew). The smoke rose up through the limbs and became suspended, as if dangling, clinging to the palms of needles and slowly sifting skyward. It was an incredibly clear night, more stars were visible in the narrow stretch of sky above the river than on any wide-open western night I have ever seen. The air is getting cooler for the season and, stepping away from the fire, I saw my breath escape my lungs in a solid, semi-tangible form.

We sat near the fire and roasted brats when we heard the first loud grumbling growl coming through the forest. We quickly fastened the dogs and stayed silent, just listening. The deep vibrations of snorting groans came closer as the animals approached. About fifty feet away, up the hill towards camp, they stopped and continued making a loud and aggressive sound. Shortly after, we heard another guttural growl about fifty feet downstream from us, and then heard a large animal enter the water. Then they were quiet. We thought they had left, when again the growling came from the hill, closer and louder this time. I prepared for an encounter. I stoked up the fire, removed my knife from its sheath, and walked up the trail, towards the growling beasts.

I repeated the word, "Hey," loudly and deeply. Then they were gone. We remained at the fire a while and then walked back to camp along the dark and wild forest trail.

The darkness felt more alive after our encounter. Once settled into our tent, we discussed the event. It was most likely the mother and cub bears, and we had interfered with their nightly route to water.

...

I awoke today with a splitting hangover. This was cured by Mayana's French toast with maple syrup topped by strawberries freshly picked from her garden back home. We relaxed while reading in the sanctuary for most of the day.

August 15 Monday

It is an exceptionally muggy night as I look out my tent at the approaching darkness. I had to remove my T-shirt to keep from soaking in sweat. The temperature can't be higher than seventy degrees Fahrenheit, but the humidity is exceedingly high. There's a galvanic force in the air, and when the storm comes, it will be a powerful one.

I woke up to rain, thunder, and lightning this morning, and being that I was tired and comfortably lying with my woman, it took a few moments to convince myself to go outside and tend to the rain barrels. It has been over a week since they were filled, and though the water was still suitable for dishes and bathing, cleaner water is always better. So I arose, emptied out all my barrels, scrubbed them down, then placed them back under the dripping awning. I returned to bed and fell asleep, and dreamt of my barrels being filled with clean water.

When I awoke, the sun was warming our bed. Luckily, Mayana was in no hurry, for even though it is Monday, she took the morning off, so was in no rush to get to work. When I climbed from the tent, I was disappointed to see the front rain barrel, which is the largest, completely empty. Upon closer investigation, I realized that in my haste to return to bed earlier this morning, I had slammed the barrel on a sharp log, creating a small incision at the bottom. This I patched using a piece of tarp and some canvas tear-mending solution. I'm not certain it will be water tight, but it's raining now so I will find out soon enough.

Mayana left mid-morning during an intermission in the rain. I enjoy walking through the damp forest. Everything feels more alive and potent. I spent most of the morning walking through the forest, and when I finally returned to camp, my clothes were drenched all the way through.

It is raining again as I sit in the screen house making this entry. A moment ago I heard a multitude of animals. There was one definitely large, walking down the creek bed towards the river, and was most likely a deer. Last night I dreamt of bears and woke up several times swearing there was one directly outside the tent, but quickly returned to sleep.

The rain is getting stronger and I move into the tent. The rain on my tarpaulin is a lovely sound, but it also serves to dampen the other noises of the forest that my ears are reaching for. I sit alone in my tent by lantern light, a pencil in one hand, vodka Tang in the other, with a generous pinch of chewing tobacco in my lip, wondering what good I have done in my life to deserve this luxury of solitude.

I began working on my novel again this afternoon;

it has been a week since I wrote anything. I started by rereading the first seventy pages, making additions where plausible, and then began writing a new chapter. Nine-hundred new words today. Not impressive, but a good start back into it.

Without Mayana at camp, I felt a void at the loss of her smile and conversation. Sitting down and not having her sit across from me seemed empty. But as the day went on I got back into my solitary routine, and in that state of mind I can convince myself that I am the only human alive or who has ever lived. The emptiness becomes filled with wonder. Though I must admit, without the company of Sly, I would be more inclined to lose pieces of my mind, though I rarely share much more monologue with him than to say whether I am going towards the car or the river when I leave camp, or to notify him of dinner, which he generally observes of his own accord. It is a great pleasure to have an ally here at camp. He is quite the lackadaisical ally, spending most of his day in his tent, even when the mosquitoes are mild, which I might add was not the case today. Earlier today, I went down to the river to fetch back the cooler and chairs that were left the other night. I called to Sly as I left camp, "Going to the river," and even gave him several whistles and calls as I walked down the trail. Normally he runs behind me and then passes and leads the way to the river. Not this time. Instead, he remained in his tent, imprisoned by the surrounding army of mosquitoes.

I arrived at the river and, finding everything in order, decided to sit on the log at the river's edge. It was beautiful and sunny that time of day, and the river glistened. I watched the dragonflies hover and small baitfish swim in the shallows. Then I heard Sly wailing from camp, giving the most mournful howl I have ever heard, except, perhaps, for the day he got his leg caught in a mountain lion snare while we were working in some remote Wyoming mountains. But that is another story for another time and place. So I yelled out to him, to let him know I was close, and proceeded to hustle towards camp, wondering what his emergency was. The entire walk back I called out his name, but he had become silent. I arrived to see him standing in the center of camp calmly waiting for me. Poor dog, I think he gets lonelier out here than I ever have.

Some of the asters have started to bloom; they make darling little purple and white symmetrical flowers, which are perched up on long narrow stems. I need to explore more of this land. I have hardly breeched the forest, mostly sticking to my trail and camp. I wonder what discoveries await me, what unknown species of plants and animals I have only thus far imagined. It's mostly the thought of being covered in wood ticks that prevents me from going in, or more likely, the hassle of picking hundreds of them from Sly's fur. I need to put on my tick armor and bug spray, retain Sly at camp, and then go venturing into this unknown that surrounds me.

August 16 Tuesday

Hearing the grunting, growling grumble of a slow shuffling bear has become a regular part of my nights. Tonight I walked back from the Jeep an hour before sunset, and when I was no more than fifty feet down the trail, I heard the bear behind me on the other side of our two-track. I walked directly back to the Jeep, towards the bear, to get Sly's leash and fasten him so he wouldn't give chase. I then returned to camp and put Sly in the tent.

After this, I attached my machete to my belt alongside my Buck knife. Then I did what any logical man living alone in the forest and more than sixty miles away from the nearest medical center would do—I walked towards where I'd heard the bear. It has been too long of him parading through the forest without introduction. My curiosity is too great, and I believe he is curious about me as well. It is time we meet.

I sauntered slowly and low in my camouflage, bending with the shape of a tree, and only placing steps during a gust of wind so the sound would mute my footings. It was dark, but I still resisted the urge to make any sudden movements, such as slapping the mosquitoes from my flesh or flicking the spider from my shirt. I wanted to become the forest.

It was only natural that while engaged in this chase I imagined myself a great bear hunter. I have no reason to kill the bear, but there was still that instinct, and I imagined a great battle between man and beast.

I spent three hours of darkness creeping through the trees. At one point, I heard what I believed to be the bear. It came as a series of loud crunches moving fast across the forest floor, originating less than fifty feet away and moving the opposite direction. I returned to camp without seeing my prey.

I now believe there are two sets of bears that frequent this landscape: a mother and cub who approach from the south and pass through the property to the north (most likely the ones that approached us the other night by the river) and another single bear, most likely a male and possibly the father of the cub, who comes from the west, going east through our land, likely following the creek bed most of the way towards the river.

...

I am back at camp, standing near the fire, and it is difficult to hear past the crackling flames, so I step away into the dark. Shortly after stepping away from the fire, straining my ears to hear if the bear was near, I was surrounded by mosquitoes. It is even more difficult to hear past their screaming attack than it is to hear past the fire, so I stepped back into the radius of smoke. I then heard an owl hoot from a tree nearby and several coyotes yapping in the distance.

At this point, Sly was getting restless in the tent, so I let him out, only then realizing he was after a mouse that was scuttling around outside the tent. I let him have some fun while I went back to the fire to listen. It was a while before I heard the bear again, making his way west towards where he'd come from.

I settled the fire into a position I knew would not escape the rock ring and then let it burn while I came into the tent. All around me are noises loud and soft, near and far. I let my imagination wander into images of what they might be. Two wolves howled someplace to the north. Now another one slightly to the west of them. The night is full of song and mystery.

One of these days, I would like to explore the woods during daylight while the animals are asleep, and it is me disturbing their dreams instead of vice versa. I have no doubt that the animals are more terrified of men than we are of them. We have caused much more cruelty, disruption and destruction to their world compared to what they have done to ours. Perhaps, like any conquered species, there are a few renegades that await their opportunity for revenge, but I'm quite certain most of them only wish to avoid us.

On to other topics. I didn't do much more than sit around camp today, for I fell into a writing spree. Approximately 2,250 words. These words developed a new scene and got the story rolling again. Currently I am at 27,000 words total. I am aiming for a finished book of 250 pages. These words in my present format are placing me at 117 pages. I'm approximately two-fifths done with the story that I have in mind. It feels like I'm on track. I still have roughly six weeks at camp to finish it.

August 17 Wednesday

Tonight I sat outside and listened to the bear make his regular tour through the forest. The longer I remain still, the more mosquitoes that gather in brigades around my head for a screaming contest. It's amazing how loud these little buggers can be. I sat in full pants, raincoat, and mosquito netting, so only my hands were exposed, and these I overlapped so only one was available.

All I want now is to see the bear. I'm growing tired of these specter engagements. I need to put an image in my eyes to understand him. He doesn't seem to be interested in approaching my camp, so I will spend more time seeking him out.

Sly has acted anxious and playful all day. On our walk up to the Jeep to call Mayana, he dashed ravenously into the trees, and a grouse flew up from its roost. He doesn't hear a single thing I say to him once he's on the hunt.

I've noticed patches of a pearlescent white, cylindrical plant curved like a candy cane, growing at the base of trees around camp. I opened up a field guide and identified them as Indian pipe. It's actually a fungus, but in the spring can produce a beautiful flower, which is rare for fungi. I also read up on mosquitoes, wondering if these small rain puddles that form in camp were supporting larvae and adding to my discomfort. I learned that from the time an egg is deposited to the time an adult emerges is generally three to five weeks, and that they need very little water to support this cycle. I should start draining the puddles to reduce the population. I also learned that, like the horsefly, only the females feast on blood, while the males seek out plant nectar. This makes sense, since the female requires blood to produce an egg, and the male needs nectar to produce its fertilizer, or as it is, to pollinate the egg. I wonder if humans have it all wrong. We generally associate meat eating with big burly men and salads with fine wiry women. Perhaps our diet is backwards, and our species would be more balanced if it were the women who were known for eating large bloody steaks.

I woke up fairly early this morning but lay in bed for a couple hours contemplating my novel. I've been thinking about the ending — or rather, the part just before the ending — more than the part I'm presently working on. I will not write that part yet, but rather let it ferment, so it is more fully developed when I get there. I wrote 4,500 words today, which is my high for a single day, and I worked for five hours. It's odd to imagine a stranger reading my work; I wonder what they will think of my tale. I hope it is a success; it would be a great life to spend my summers out here writing and my winters in town working in my woodshop. I try not to think of these things yet; I cannot be distracted by grandiose delusions. Or can I? If my book fails, I will be perfectly happy finding another job and living a simple life with Mayana.

I am out of vodka but there are a few beers in the cooler. I am hungry but will wait until morning and enjoy a Clif bar. Beer is fodder for the lonely man's appetite.

August 18 Thursday

Not a very hot day, but extremely muggy. I spent most of it in my screen house with my shirt off and my pants open. I imagine this sight would have caused some suspicion if anyone had walked into camp.

I am now able to crush mosquitoes out of the air in the dark. I have become a full-fledged mosquito assassin. I'm not sure that I'm happy to have developed this skill. The presence of mosquitoes was light today. Earlier, I was able to sit outside for nearly two full minutes before getting attacked. Perhaps word of my abilities have traveled through their populace, and now they are afraid of me. Having fewer of them has encouraged Sly to spend more time outside of his sanctuary.

Today I read a poorly written book by a local author. I will exclude the name and title out of kindness. While reading the book I often cursed audibly at the fumbling sentences. I did learn something though; if a book this terrible can be published, then mine has a shot. The only question is, will people enjoy it? The closer I get to finishing, the more these thoughts are on my mind. I wonder if this other author believed he had fashioned a great novel. I will not get ahead of myself, but instead focus on the plot, live inside of it, and let the story grow in my mind.

Today I woke up and didn't want to write. I only had four beers last night so there was no hangover to blame. I considered spending the day kayaking, or fishing, or taking an exploratory hike, but this is my job, to write, and work must come first. I needed to challenge myself, get some motivation, so it was agreed between myself and myself that if I wrote 2,000 words, I would be rewarded with a drive to the Effie Café for fresh pizza.

I started my work by rereading much of the story, and struggled for new words. Then I noticed a glow develop around my periphery, and this three-dimensional world built a new layer. That fourth dimension of vision was the imaginary place my eyes could see which laminated reality. As I explored this new dimension, the ambient world melded with the past, and the imagination manipulated both to create something different. I was in a trance, as if blacked-out, and unaware of what I was doing.

Several hours later I stood up to toss my knife and pace around because I wanted to separate myself for a while and refocus. When I returned to the computer I was surprised to see that I'd added 3,250 words. I reread them and they were good. Perhaps I should blackout more often.

Before I got up to leave for the Café, I heard rustling beside the sanctuary. I looked over to see a weasel approaching. I remained calm and quiet. He came within two feet of me before looking into my eyes and darting away. He continued to dart back and forth, seemingly curious and probably hungry. He was unafraid until I got up to leave. That's the closest I have ever come to a weasel. I considered tossing him some bread, domesticating him, making a friend, but decided that if he got too comfortable with me, he was more vulnerable to getting attacked by Sly.

I got to the Jeep and put the key into the ignition. It is only nine miles to Effie. It is only nine miles, but there are so many trees and animals between. I sat in the Jeep with the engine off and thought about pizza. I thought about the little food I had at camp, and the melted cheese, hot sauce, spicy pork, and chewy dough sounded appealing. Then I thought about this journal, or rather, I thought about the future. I imagined reading it at some faraway date, and I knew that I would be disappointed to read how I'd succumbed to a temptation as easy as pizza.

Darkness was dropping out of the light when I stepped from my Jeep. I took a few moments to call Mayana, and while doing so, I heard the bear less than two-hundred feet to the north and already on my side of the driveway. I put Sly on a leash for the walk back so he wouldn't give chase. He heard the bear also and was excited. I could tell he was excited because he put his hunting face on, with pointed ears, large smile, raised shoulders, and rapid breath. I don't think he's ever seen a bear. I wonder if he might think it a cow. Either way, I'm sure he would enjoy the chase until he caught it.

Tomorrow is Friday, which means my woman returns. It also means I need to clean camp, cut firewood, and take a shower. It also means she'll bring me treats, herself being one of them. I would like to get some fishing in as well, but first I must write. Tomorrow my goal will be one-thousand words, a low and attainable goal, which would put my weekly total above twelve-thousand. If I can accomplish this and still have time for the chores, my reward will be fishing.

...

I spent the last 40 percent of my computer's battery listening to music. This was the first time I have played music since arriving in the forest. I decided this would be a suitable reward in exchange for the pizza. I knew I would miss pizza, but I never thought I would miss music so much. It's amazing how we can express ourselves through the lyrics and instruments of strangers. The greatest accomplishment for me would be to perform this same feat with my writing.

Now that it is silent, I hear all the animals in this nocturnal world stirring about me. I wonder what they thought of the music. Did they dance? Did it fill them with any sort of exuberance? Don't all animals make music? It certainly didn't scare them away. I wish I could listen to it all night long, but the battery is drained.

August 19 Friday

I did not complete my goal; at about one-hundred new words, I fell extremely short. I was unable to focus. No fishing today. I've never been able to write on Fridays at camp; my mind is filled with too much reality to be creative—the reality of Mayana visiting, that another person exists in this world and will be sharing this forest, and that I must be presentable for her. That's all right. Four days a week for another five weeks will be ample time to finish my novel.

I spent most of the day cleaning up camp and tossing my knife around. I'm getting good at sticking the blade into anything within fifteen feet, so I tried a longer distance. I selected a tree with an eight inch diameter and paced twenty feet away. I imagined the knife's rotation as it spun through the air. I flipped it up and held the blade end, and then launched it. The throw looked good and it hit blade first but at an odd angle that caused it to deflect off the tree and shoot straight towards the tent. Here it penetrated perfectly and tore a five inch seam in the canvas. I located my mending kit to fix the tear and decided that was enough knife throwing for today.

I began to prepare a shower. I used a four gallon aluminum brew kettle filled with rainwater. I checked the water several days ago and it looked clean. Today the water was still clear, but now there were hundreds of mosquito eggs attached to the sides and bottom of the pail. The lid doesn't fit quite tight, so there is just enough space for these bastards to sneak in and lay their eggs. I emptied the water, cleaned the pail, and then refilled it with water from another pail that looked better. Then I proceeded to heat up the water over the propane stove.

Taking a shower always satisfies me. I made it extra

warm this time and used more water than I generally do. Just as I started to rinse, a loud wind came and shook the trees. I thought of a tree blowing down onto me, and Mayana arriving to find my naked body dead and pinched to the ground. The wind has since calmed. It looks like rain, but so far, I have only heard distant thunder.

The songs of the birds have changed. I no longer hear those pleasant notes of the phoebe, which had been so common. Now there are new notes of new birds I've yet to identify. I rarely see the birds, for the forest is thick and they are constantly hidden. It would be nice to have a larger clearing where I could sit and watch them. Some of the songs I've heard are unmistakable—the loon, the eagle, and the raven—but then there are many more I do not know.

Mayana will arrive soon, so I will get some reading in and attempt to look wild and sophisticated when she arrives.

August 20 Saturday

It rained on and off most of the day. We spent the majority of our time in the screen house reading. Saturdays. It's difficult to beat the opportunity for nothingness. Sometime around mid-afternoon, when the rain gave us an interlude beneath grey skies, we sauntered into the woods. We started by the river and took the animal trail to our property line, then zig-zagged through the thickets and trees all the way back to the driveway. We saw many new parts of the property and were likely the first humans to walk this ground in many years. It is a thick jungle full of hidden treasures. We discovered several giant oak trees rising to the clouds. Even though these were the tallest trees around, we couldn't see them until they were right in front of us. We found many flattened patches of grass where the deer had lay. I had my sense of orientation the entire time, guiding towards new waypoints as we went, but it was easy to get the sensation of being lost beneath a sunless sky, engulfed in thick undergrowth and surrounded by tall trees. The forest is a captivating place. There's much of our property we haven't seen and maybe never will.

There are a lot of projects I would like to take on. Small natural projects to enhance our observation of the pristinity of this place. The next one may be to create a small path with my machete that goes down the hill from camp towards the creek bed, and then find a flat spot where I can build a log bench and we can sit to watch for critters passing.

I'm hoping the weather is good tomorrow so we can get out for a canoe ride. Our watercrafts haven't been getting much use. It's difficult during the week because most of my time is spent writing, and when I do want to take a break, I have to leave Sly locked in his tent. This I don't mind doing for a couple hours, except he howls and whines so loud that anyone within a five mile radius will think it is a wounded wolf making its death cry.

The Indian pipe is growing fast; this may be my favorite plant in the forest. The asters are in bloom and the goldenrod is blossoming. Every time I walk the driveway, I pick a dozen raspberries. It would be possible for me to live out here from fish, grouse, raspberries, hazelnuts, and wild strawberries. Perhaps next year…

We played a game of Scrabble tonight with the sound of wolves howling. Have I mentioned this is a great life?

August 21 Sunday

It's difficult to identify a favorite day or week or weekend, but this weekend has certainly been a contender.

Today we spent the morning sipping coffee and reading. It rained all night, so when the sky finally cleared early afternoon, we took the dogs for a canoe ride. This was the first time all four of us had been in the canoe. Canyon obediently jumped in and sat where we told him. Sly stepped in one side and quickly out the other. After chasing him down and dragging him back, we held him in the canoe and shoved off. We paddled a couple miles upstream and then turned around and drifted back.

We returned to camp and settled into some more reading. *Leisure* was the word of the day. Later on, we played a couple games of Scrabble. Afterwards, we had a campfire and ate some brats.

I am anxious to start writing again. Having two days without it, I get filled with new ideas. I only hope I can reproduce them with the same effect as their initial imaginings.

August 22 Monday

I woke up early this morning to see Mayana off to work. It's getting light much later as the sun begins its winter migration. It was still dark when I got back to camp, and I finished reading *Look Homeward, Angel* by Thomas Wolfe. It was long and mostly boring, but it was written with such eloquence and imagination that by the end it became one of my favorite novels. I brewed coffee and spent many long moments in a trance watching the shadows rise from their nocturnal slumber. Around mid-morning, I did some writing, but my thoughts were scattered. It was cloudy so I had difficulty keeping my laptop charged without draining the solar batteries.

A storm rolled in fast and strong. The forest was filled with electricity like the ceiling of a bumper car arena. There were echoes of thunder in the trees like stomping buffalo hooves in a stampede. I promptly went to detach all solar equipment so not to invite a lightning strike. In my haste, I crossed the connection of two wires, and nearly started a fire. The connectors and the wires were damaged, rendering them useless. My options are to either stay at camp on a stormy day without being able to write, or go to town and buy new materials. I didn't want to go to town, but it was only Monday, so if I didn't, I would be unable to write for the entire week until Mayana arrived Friday with new materials. This was the second time I was leaving camp, and I didn't like it.

I walked through the wet forest, and when I got to the Jeep, it wouldn't start. The battery was fully drained. I walked back to camp for my large solar battery and hauled that up to the Jeep for a jump-start. I knew it was dangerous in the rain, but it looked like rain all day and there was no other option. The solar battery had a charge of 11.4 volts, but I wasn't sure if this would be sufficient. It took a while, but eventually I was able to get enough charge to start the car battery. I loaded Sly into the Jeep and we drove off. Halfway through the drive the sky cleared to a beautiful day, and I wished I were back at camp.

I returned to our home in town to find the grass up to my shins. The mower had been nonfunctional, so Mayana hadn't been able to keep up. I decided while in town to make preparations for our wedding, which is only a month away. The oil in the Jeep needs to be changed, and the Matrix, Mayana's car, requires some minor repair. I have made peace with the fact that I will be in town for the next two days. This is an uncomfortable peace only agreed to with a strong sense of opposition. I intend to make the most of my time and dedicate at least five hours a day to writing. If I can reach the ten-thousand word mark this week, I will remain on track. Maybe a change of scenery will give me new inspiration and enhance the book. Tonight I sit on the back porch and am stricken by a sense of despondency. Tomorrow I will work hard and fast to accomplish my city chores so I may return to camp. I no longer feel at home in the comfort of a house.

Where is the bear? Why no sound of wolves howling? There are no mice clawing up my walls. It is too bright to be so late. How many worlds are there?

August 23 Tuesday

I wonder what footsteps walk through my camp. What tracks will remain upon my return? Does the bear use a different route when I am away? Does the weasel crawl from his den earlier in the night? Do the wolves still howl or is that only for me? Will the mice bother clawing at the walls of my tent if I am not there to disturb? Here in the city, I dream of the forest while I am awake.

I got some writing done, but not as much as I would have liked. I am less productive amongst these civil disturbances. I was alone all day and never left the house, but I felt the presence of people surrounding me. I have become dissociated. I used to be the socialite, the party thrower, the one whose presence other people suckled from. Perhaps they sucked me dry and I have nothing left to give. I bet you didn't know that about my past, did you dear journal friend? Of course not; you only know what I've told you. Don't feel neglected, though; most people never take the time to know more than they are told. How lost we are.

Mayana came home during lunch and made an egg, cheese, and brat scramble; this summer is the season of the brat. This one was missing something more than the smoky flavor; there was no mosquito topping and there was no bear begging in the darkness.

This evening we ordered our wooden wedding rings. I ordered my wedding attire from Cabela's while Mayana began the search for hers. I am going with the safari theme, while she plays the 1920's doll. How lucky we are that two eccentrics found each other.

Tomorrow I travel back to camp, alone.

...

I smell the forest. The forest is in me. I am in the forest. It is as green and silent as I remember. Have I ever been anywhere else? When I'm in the city, I think I could never leave, and when I'm in the forest, I never want to be anywhere else.

August 24 Wednesday

I arrived to find camp just as I left it. Where is the bear, the wolf, the eagle, the deer? The trees answer solemnly: here, they say, they have always been here. Where have you been? The trees ask. Lost, is all I can explain. For where else can we be found but alone in a forest? Where else can a man fully exist? Not in the city, with its cumbersome crowds. Not in a job, with its clockwork design. Only here, where he has always been. I am glad to be home.

After settling in, I sat in the screen house finishing a book by John McPhee, *Encounters with the Archdruid*. I was surrounded not only by the songs of new birds, but also the sight. I am not certain if my prolonged absence invited them closer to camp, or if it is their time for migration, and they would have been here regardless. Of the birds I saw today, I was able to identify the goldfinch, yellow warbler, and pileated woodpecker, all viewable from the sanctuary. The squirrels have also braved themselves closer to my dwelling.

I have been here eight hours and am yet to see a mosquito. Where am I? This is the way the forest should be. Though it may be too easy.

I have been sitting by a small fire with beer that I brought from town. The difference between having three beers remaining and two beers remaining is gargantuan, oceanic even. With three beers left, I feel as though the night is young and I am at liberty to drink away. With two beers left, I feel that the end is near, I can see the finish line, and I must pace myself if I desire this ride to continue. There are now two beers left. It is getting dark. I sit beside a fire with enough wood to last the night.

It is a sport I play here alone with my thoughts, and the score is, Beer: 0, Me: 9.

I saw eyes in the forest. They were looking at me.

August 25 Thursday

I took a shower today, the first since last Friday. I don't ever feel dirty, but the shower felt good. Makes me realize how much water I waste taking one or two long hot showers a day in town. We have the ability to live comfortably with much less than what we normally take advantage of.

Tomorrow I must get some physical exercise.

I was swatting at my tent ceiling, trying to rid it of the mice that were climbing outside, when the noise startled a bear who gave a short, loud growl nearby. Then a single wolf gave a long mournful howl into the night sky. Now Sly has awakened from his slumber and wants to go outside, but I will keep him in. Too many unknowns for him to chase out there.

I will now read myself to sleep.

August 26 Friday

What a glorious day. During the past two days, I have only seen half a dozen mosquitoes. After weeks of suffering and turmoil, I find peace. I doubt it will last. It has been windy, which could be the cause of my comfort. I'm hoping it is a sign of the changing season. Not because I'm anxious for autumn. Even though I love autumn, it's a sign of winter, which is a sign of my departure. But even though I want the summer to last, summer is the season of the mosquito, and for that reason alone, I am ready for it to be finished.

I saw two pileated woodpeckers today. They were close, loudly pounding on trees above our fern garden, less than fifty feet from my rousting place in the sanctuary. I snuck over to the tent to fetch my camera and then crept back towards them for a picture, but they became aware of my presence and promptly flew from sight. I was able to clearly identify one as a male and the other a female. The male has a full red forehead and a red "mustache," while the female only has red on the tip of her head.

I had a productive day, 3,600 new words, which is more than the combined total of the two days spent in town last week. There are too many distractions at the house, and I am a sucker for them all. Here I have no distractions. There are other things I could do, such as cut wood, build a shed, clear trails, explore the forest, fish, and kayak, but writing is my purpose; my purpose is to produce something substantial for more eyes and minds than my own. I want what perhaps every writer has ever wanted—for strangers to read my words and find a piece of themselves, to be both mystified and fulfilled, to understand. I realized that the origin and substance of every novel is in a single thought, every other word on every other page is decoration. The decoration is the fun part, but it is important not to let the decoration get so thick that it becomes a disguise.

The forest is filled with animal activity, most of which I never see, so I am thankful every chance I get to witness some of it, however small or seemingly insignificant. Today there were several mice and a few frogs hiding in the cool chamber of my food cache. It's funny, at any house in the world, or even any yard, the sign of a rodent would be taken as a threat, and all resources available would be applied towards its extermination.

It's shameful to be a part of such behavior, but then I have to ask myself, could a population of six billion plus people occupy this planet and survive as I am now? As a member of nature, not above it? Unlikely.

Outside, I hear the growling of a bear. It sounds close.

I don't care. I have been listening to music. I reread all 172 pages of my story tonight. I am over halfway done.

Sly wants to go out, but I won't let him. Danger awaits in the darkness. So we will sit in the tent as I read myself to sleep from the pages of Aldo Leopold.

I drank more than I intended to tonight, but that is okay; in the morning I will drink much water and be ready.

August 27 Saturday

Nature's greatest delusion is making men feel best when doing what's worst. That is because nature does not want us here and so uses reverse psychology to trick us into an inebriated state of self-destruction. At least that was the thought I woke up with as I pulled myself from bed with a terrible hangover. Last night I felt brilliant and indestructible. A genius in the night becomes a fool the next morning. I drank much vodka and was still asleep when Mayana arrived late this morning. She had a work meeting last night and so couldn't drive here as she generally does on Fridays.

I spent most of the day at roughly 30 percent functionality. Mayana thought this was funny and mocked me accordingly. This didn't stop her from performing her usual feats of creating delicious campfire cookeries. I ate steak and drank wine and tonight finally felt good again.

We spent the evening by the river and saw a shooting star. It was a wonderful night to be in the forest, but they all have been. She said our wedding rings had arrived in the mail, and I realized there wasn't much time left for me here. Soon I will be a married man and that makes me happy. Soon I will be a domesticated man and that makes me rebellious.

August 28 Sunday

Mayana slept most of the day in the open air of the sanctuary. I brought my laptop to the river and produced 3,800 new words. This time I cooked dinner; it was brats and canned corn with vodka and Tang. Delicious.

She leaves early for work tomorrow, so we will now lay in bed and read by lantern light.

August 29 Monday

Earlier today I was in the sanctuary writing. It had been extremely windy all day so the sound of rustling leaves and snapping branches became regular and unnoticed. Then I heard two successive loud snaps near me, so I looked up. There, only sixty feet away, was the large black hump of the bear's back, riding above the top of ferns like the crest of a whale breaking through the surface of the sea. It was moving towards me. In a flash of excitement, I stood up, removed my knife from its sheath, and exited the screen house while walking crouched down. My next thought was of Sly. I looked over and the bear was now rushing in the opposite direction. Sly was in his tent, so I quickly zipped him in. I looked back into the ferns but didn't see the bear. I rushed into the tent and grabbed my camera, then approached the edge of the ferns. I couldn't see it, I couldn't hear it. I knelt down for a better view — nothing. I slowly walked into the ferns, stepping as softly as I could. About thirty feet away a loud clambering shook the trees. The bear ran from me, knocking over a dead tree in the process. I watched the tops of the smaller trees parting like waves as it fled into the forest. I stood still a while, camera in one hand, knife in the other, but the bear was gone into the wilderness.

It was good to finally see the bear, though I am concerned about him being comfortable enough to approach my camp during daylight. I have seen bears before, either on a trail, from a canoe, or through the window of a moving car. It is an entirely different experience to know that they live amongst me. Nothing but a thin canvas wall protects me in the night. Though, after this encounter, I am quite certain this particular bear will be scared off for a while.

These large wild bears fear us more than we fear them. That was a fact easy to believe while living in a city, but after a couple months living alone in bear country, it is more of an unanswered question. I reminded myself that they have been the target of near extermination, that man has hunted them wherever they roam. I imagine the tables turned, and it was man who was hunted in his natural habitat by the invasive bear. I don't want the bear to fear me, I don't want to fear the bear, and I certainly don't want one in my camp. Unless he's bringing me fresh fish.

Other animals have grown comfortable with me as well. This afternoon a Franklin's ground squirrel came right up to the screen house, about an arm's reach away. These are really marvelous looking squirrels. They have a speckled body with a long, narrow grey-white tail and a pale face. The temptation to feed him was strong, but I refrained. He darted off as soon as Sly emerged from the tent.

A fairly good day writing, 2,600 new words. I've been trying to wrap up Part I, but every time I think it's close, it gets further away. It is difficult to eliminate details that seem important to the story, just for the sake of brevity. This book may be longer than I initially anticipated.

The mosquitoes continue to be mild. Only now as the sun is setting have I gotten my first bite in three days.

I called Mayana last night. I almost wrote her name as "Lamara," which is the name of the lead female character in my novel. She said she bought her wedding dress today. It's awkward being out here alone, having a fiancée living in a city making all these decisions and purchases without me.

Now that I have seen the bear, and seen him flee from me, I want to stalk him in the night. I want to find his lair and study him. I want to follow him through the dark and hidden passages of the forest. I want to learn from him how to be as wild and as free.

I just heard a choir of wolves howling from the north. I love this wild land and this wild life. This is the best investment ever, and it cost roughly the same price as a new SUV. Imagine if I were out driving a fancy new SUV on the city streets, instead of here in the forest alone. What a waste that would be. I would never have known the presence of the bear or the soft sound of a forest breeze coming across a gentle river. It would have been difficult to get so far into my novel while driving. The stars shine above me now, and not a cloud to interfere. Out here they are as old as they ever have been, but so bright and young. There is not an SUV in the world with a better view.

August 30 Tuesday

Today I walked down into the ferns where I saw the bear. After close examination, I was able to distinguish the path he had walked into camp. It was difficult to locate, because here he had walked leisurely, unaware of my presence. The path exiting camp was more obvious, as he had rushed away, unconcerned with being silent.

Today I have been hearing gunshots in the distance. It is difficult to judge the location, but likely two to five miles away. This is a reminder that hunting season is approaching. I wish I could tell all of the local wildlife to take refuge here on our land. I am not anti-hunting in any way; I believe it is the purest form of gathering a meal. In my opinion, killing an animal for sustenance is no different than picking an apple from a tree—both are fundamental methods of organic energy exchange. But I enjoy the sight, sound, and company of wildlife enough to want to safeguard them as much as possible. The more wildlife that exist here, the wilder this place becomes. If the bear I saw yesterday were to be shot, how long, if ever, would it be until I was privileged enough to see one again in this forest? Is there a line of bears waiting to take over his territory, or would it be years before a new one discovered it?

When it's dark, every shadow in the forest looks like a bear. Earlier, I heard loud crashing branches near the creek. Because the bear fled from me yesterday, I felt brave enough to investigate. By the time my loud feet reached the creek, there was nothing to see. It was most likely a deer.

August 31 Wednesday

Last night I lay awake with an uneasy mind. Long after dark, I started seeing lightning in the distance. This kept me awake longer. The lightning was quick to get close. The sky filled with powerful electricity and extremely loud thunder. I could tell it was going to be an admirable storm. I gathered up my laptop, headlamp, blanket, and a book. I put Sly on a leash and traveled up the dark trail to the Jeep. I was uncertain if I would spend the remainder of the night in the Jeep, or drive to town. I waited for the weather to decide for me. By the time I got to the Jeep, the lightning was above me in furious magnitude, so close that the thunder seemed to come before the light. There were many flashes with high intensity, and looking into this night sky could blind me quicker than staring at the sun. I had yet to see a single raindrop, and there was not a rustle in the leaves. I have seen tornadoes approach like this, so I readied myself to leave, but decided I was as safe in a parked car as a moving one, so I kicked back to enjoy the show. By the time the thunder went silent and the storm passed, the sky was brightening. Above the rising sun on the far horizon, I could see the pulsating storm high in the sky. I walked back to camp and fell asleep to daylight.

I awoke early afternoon and walked to the road to call Mayana. She was concerned, for the same storm had wreaked havoc in Bemidji, falling many trees and blowing down billboards. After I had assured her that I was all right, and she had assured me that she and our house were the same, I returned to camp to write.

I finished Part I today. There are a couple of scenes that I may delete, and I'm sure that as I develop Part II and Part III, I will need to add further backstory, but I'm moving forward.

After writing, I cut enough firewood for the weekend. For this task, I never have to go far, just to the edge of the forest. I drag out a couple of dead trees, generally selecting those that have been dangling from the branches of other living trees, for they have had time to dry above the wet and decomposing forces of the soil.

I then cleared a trail from the shower down to the creek bed. Here there were numerous deer tracks, one of them quite large. This will be a good place to sit up at night and watch for wildlife. I returned the machete to its holster and walked to camp. I was reminded that camp is on a good-sized hill, about sixty feet of incline in forty feet of distance. I thought about the mountains and I remembered the way my legs burned after spending a day in them. I missed that pain because it made me stronger, so I proceeded to jog up and down the hill by camp a dozen times. This helped, and now I am ready for a book and vodka.

September 1 Thursday

Keeping my cooler buried below ground with a piece of plywood over top does increase the longevity of the ice and prevent larger animals from raiding my supplies, but every time I open up the lid to my food cache, I am presented with the sight of worms, spiders, toads, and mice. Living in a proper city home, any one of these in proximity to a food supply would be cause for alarm and would likely result in the purchase of poisons or a call to the exterminator. Considering my present location, I choose to ignore them. In reality, I could eat any of these pests. There is no real threat in their presence, so I change my mind about them being a symbol of poor sanitary conditions, and view them as the opposite, as indicators of a great food source — my food source.

My normal food routine is a Clif bar around mid-morning, instant coffee all day, a beer or two around early evening, and then pasta and meat for dinner. These Mayana prepares every week before her visit and brings to me frozen. It's really quite luxurious for a man living alone in the wild, but I am not here as a test of surviving off the land, but rather surviving with the land as a solitary member confronting isolation in the quest of confronting my own mind and writing about that experience. The real challenge is the isolation and enforcing my own motivation. Every day I must push myself to write instead of spending the day in leisure. Every day I must remind myself that my time here is brief, and that I worked hard to have this opportunity, and it will be better in the end if I have an accomplishment to show for it. Every day I must harness the feeling of loneliness and utilize this as fuel for creativity. But I do spend ample time in leisure.

September 2 Friday

I prefer to stay awake all night and fall asleep to the songs of morning birds. Lack of sleep can be powerful because it keeps the mind from processing information through dreams, and so this same information is left to the imagination of conscious thoughts. I drank vodka last night until the bottle was dry and then brewed a pot of coffee and drank it all while writing. I generally don't work on my novel after dark due to the inability of my solar panels to charge the laptop. I drained my laptop battery and then plugged it in to the solar power system and drained all three of the deep-cycle batteries. It will be difficult to bring these back up to full charge with the autumn sun traveling lower on the horizon and getting less photons to the solar panels, but it was worthwhile. I wrote some of my best work while fueled by coffee and vodka. My memory was in full harmony with the present, and the words came out before I even thought about them. Inebriation doesn't fuel creativity, but it weakens the power of doubt and so provides clarity.

I slept in the hammock much of the day and awoke to the sound of chipmunk chatter. I returned to camp and forced myself to cut firewood so I would be ready for Mayana's visit. It began to storm so I stood outside and let the rain soak my clothes through to the flesh. Rainwater has a conducive power, as if the earth is returning to my body, and I can feel it soothe my entire being. If ever again I live in a city home, I will make an effort to be outside during the storms instead of wasting them beneath a roof.

September 3 Saturday

Last night after the rain, we had a long campfire and burned most of the wood I thought would last through the weekend. Sometime shortly after dark, we heard a pack of wolves howling. They were the closest I've heard them and sounded to be near the western edge of our property, less than three-hundred feet away. We heard many more vocal notes at this proximity. Later on, I gave a sarcastic howl to the quiet night. Mayana followed with a realistic howl. Instantly after her howl into the dark, we heard the wolf pack howl from even nearer than before, as if they were answering her and coming for a visit. The dogs were secured in the tent, but I could hear them shuffling their feet anxiously. I stepped away from the fire so that I could see better and knelt down on the edge of camp, hoping to spot one. They were definitely close because we could hear their playful chatter, which was much quieter than the howls. They must have killed a deer, or perhaps the bear, for I woke up several times in the night to hear them making various vocal sounds: some growls, some howls, some whimpers, and some playful.

Last night we named our new trail that leads from camp to the small creek. This creek has been dry for most of my time here, only flowing after a rain. We imagined a beaver on reconnaissance finding this dry riverbed and becoming disheartened. The trail is now known as the "Brokenhearted Beaver Trail."

Today was spent on the shores of pristine waters. We spent most of the morning by our river, watching birds and butterflies. Then we took an exploratory drive and stopped at several nearby lakes. I tried fishing at one with no success. It's as if these warm-water species are mocking me for having spent the previous six years in trout streams. I had refined my trout fishing technique and was experiencing high success rates, and now I must relearn how to fish for different species. We stopped at a lake several miles east of here; it was calm and beautiful, and we saw two speckled fawns prancing across a meadow.

Now we are back at camp for dinner and a game of Scrabble. If the rain holds off, we may go for a late night paddle.

September 4 Sunday

Last night the wolves howled from nearby again. There sounded to be six or seven at the place where they howled from the previous night, and then two others at a greater distance who returned their calls. I presume that the larger pack is on a hunt, or in this case, returning to a kill, and the other two are at the den, possibly looking over this year's litter of pups. The only prey that seems large enough to return a second night would be a bear or moose. Incidentally, the location that I heard their howls was approximately the same place where I would first hear the bear begin his nightly tour.

We arose earlier than usual today. After breakfast, we pulled a couple chairs into the fern garden. Mayana sketched in her notepad while I finished a book by Aldo Leopold. This afternoon, I went out in the kayak to cast large flies for muskie. Two consecutive days fishing without a catch. I need to forget what I learned trout fishing in Wyoming and remember my warm-water techniques. There are fish in this river; one of these days, I will start catching them. I need to fish deeper.

Tonight we took a late night paddle up the river, and left the dogs at camp. We heard Sly howling from camp while we were over a mile upstream. This served as a good comparison to judge the distance of the wolf howls at night. We paddled quietly into the setting sun, hoping for animal sightings. We turned around at the red barn and drifted back to camp. Immediately after dark, we were surrounded by an acrobatic swarm of bats. There were hundreds of them flying low in the river corridor. There was also an emergence of snowy-white caddisflies, and the bats were enjoying the feast.

They flew close to us before turning away, and we felt the beating of their wings.

I thought about the time when I was young, and a swarm of bats came out of our fireplace into the house. We were able to secure the glass doors of the fireplace and trap most of them, but a dozen flew off into the house. We spent hours stalking them and killing them with brooms and towels. We thought we had them all until a week later one was spotted and promptly killed. I killed them without a second thought while they were in our house as intruders, but here in the wild, I enjoyed their presence and was truly amazed to be amongst them.

After the paddle, we walked up the dark trail to camp. We will finish the evening reading in bed. Tomorrow Mayana leaves to her separate life, and I will stay here in mine. I would like to go back with her, but there's only one month left of good weather, and I've got work to do and a forest to observe.

September 5 Monday

I wrote 5,300 words today, which is a single day's best. The story marches on and my mind is split into three spheres. The first sphere is reality, or rather the forest and my life here. The second sphere is my novel, and while working on it, this becomes my reality. The third is writing this journal, and it is often difficult to restrain my imagination and focus on writing the actual events of the day. I am split into three spheres, and I value them all equally.

Only two and a half weeks until the wedding, and I intend to spend the rest of it here finishing my novel. Better keep working.

The smell of campfire covers my hands. The sounds of wolves fill my ears. The sight of freedom decorates my eyes. I am home. Sly enjoys it here as much as I. He carries a different face when in the wild. He is always excited to chase any sound of the forest, and there were plenty of sounds today. Recently, all the little critters of the forest have become comfortable frequenting our camp. It takes a few chases from Sly before the squirrel, chipmunk, weasel, frog, or bird realizes he is as a threat.

···

I've been thinking about Wyoming a lot lately. It's difficult to grasp places that exist, places where I have been, where so much was experienced and learned, where I may never return in this life. It makes me realize I must take advantage of my surroundings while I am surrounded by them.

I only saw one mosquito today. Just before dark, there was an emergence of caddisflies from the river. The raspberry brambles are fruitless. The blue bead lilies are beginning to whither. The ferns are turning yellow and brown. The predominate colors come from the bunchberries, and the flowers of asters, daisies, birdsfoot trefoil, St. John's wort, goldenrod, and butter and eggs. Soon the forest will be a vibrant orange and purple and red. Soon the days will be short, and the nights will be cold. Soon the forest will sleep. I sleep alone in the forest. So I drink. I sing verses of songs that I know to the stillness of deep night. I read verses from stories that I've written and those written by strangers, and feel as though I live inside of them.

September 6 Tuesday

Lately, I've been dreaming in narrations. The only thing I hear in the dreams is the voiceover of an omniscient narrator. Must be from all the writing. I added 2,300 words today. I remember being a child, and after watching a good movie, I would imagine myself as the characters. It's essentially the same as an adult writing stories alone in the forest.

It's getting dark much earlier. I sat outside reading as long as the light permitted. I am now in the tent and have heard several large branches snap. I've given up worrying about whatever is out there. If an animal decides to attack, I will deal with it when it happens. Wondering what's out there isn't going to prevent a thing. So I sit inside these canvas walls, watching the lantern shadows and thinking about what I can do to make my book the best it can be.

I've been thinking about finding a job the past few days. Probably a result of the approaching wedding combined with my camping season coming to an end. I need to erase this thought from my head so I can focus on writing; this is my job now.

September 7 Wednesday

I am consumed by the written word. If I am not involved in writing my novel, I am indulging in reading someone else's. If I am not reading the written word, I am writing in this journal. I am writing about writing. I am writing squared. I had a good day with the novel, my most productive to date, adding 6,300 new words.

I do find time to enjoy my surroundings and experience the wilderness. I often take a break from writing to wander around the forest. This generally involves either admiring new specimens of plants or throwing my knife into the ground. I often wander down to the river's edge and spend many long moments entranced by the serenity of slow-moving water.

The birds have become highly active, and I am seeing a lot more of them. A pine siskin spent most of the day within ten feet of the screen house. I saw a bald eagle fly over me then land high up in an aspen where it perched and shrieked. The chattering calls of pileated woodpeckers sounded from nearby, and I heard their echoes reverberating through the forest. The obnoxious honking of Canada geese filled the air; some of them sounded to be on the river, while others passed over in flight.

The leaves of wild sarsaparilla are turning yellow. The fruit of bunchberries and blue bead lilies are going rotten. The raspberries have dropped and withered into the soil. Acorns have fallen from the oaks, and the firs have dropped their cones. Today the sky was dark and cloudy, the air kept a nocturnal chill. Soon the forest will be bald save for the evergreens. Soon the animals will either hibernate, migrate, or battle the harsh winter. Soon the place where I now sit will have snow above my seated shoulders. Soon the water in the river will be protected by a thick skin of ice. Soon the forest will not remember my face. Soon I will have a separate home, sheltered from the cold and the harsh truths of winter, and all of this will retreat to memory.

Sly has also changed his behavior. He has adapted to wildness and senses the difficult times ahead. He has adopted the mentality of hyperphagia, spending the entire day on a hunt. Most of today he was away from camp, more so than any other day. Several times I had to get up and look for him. He would eventually come running to my calls with a big smile on his face, mud on his nose and paws, with seedpods and burs filling his fur. It is good to see his wild side.

I want to wander into the darkness. Take me, old powerful forest. Make me part of your eternal nature. I want to live in your history. Let me live with you in death forever. This is my home. This is my grave. I do not fear you. I do not wish to die anywhere else. You are my god. You are my soul. You are the brilliant manifestation of my imagination. Let me surrender myself to your arms. Let me be weak, so you can make me strong.

September 8 Thursday

The darkness is so engulfing that the screen light of my laptop sends out bright rays visible for many feet. I hear no automobile or dog bark or airplane. I smell neither pavement nor exhaust nor detergent. I see not the mowed yard or street light or television. My senses are full in the absence of these.

It is Thursday night, which means there is an adult hockey league happening in Bemidji. I only recently asked Mayana to research the hockey schedule, so that I can prepare to play when I return to town, likely in less than a month. I could be skating and scoring goals and feeling the adrenaline. I would take a good game of hockey over good sex six times out of ten, but I would take a solitary night in the forest seven.

I am addicted to the open space and my wandering thoughts. I am in love with the silence, aromas, and scenery. The sight of darkness this complete fills me with fear and I enjoy it. Fear is one of the greatest sensations because it reminds me my life is valued. Only ignorance or a life with no value can be fearless. I embrace the fear because the darkness will get me anyway, when I am due. I have had many chances to die, but so far, none of them have been worthy.

When I go, I do not want to be buried in a pine box in a family cemetery beside a church. I do not want to be cremated and have my ashes tossed into a mountain breeze. I do not want to be laid upon a burning river raft and pushed downstream.

I want to be abandoned upon the soil of this forest so that I may return to the cycle. I do not want my blood and flesh and bones to be wasted. If laid bare upon this earth, I will be available to the wolf and bird and worm. If laid bare upon this earth, I will remain here forever. Forever isn't that long because I will be forgotten. Forever can be a long time if the cycle of worm to fish to bird to wolf continues. Forever can be immortality through the life of other animals.

September 9 Friday

The forest is most intriguing on a sunny day with a mild breeze. It is then that the shadows change most frequently, creating a plethora of indescribable shapes. It is then that an autumn leaf is rustled from its parent tree and sounds like footsteps in the forest as it slowly tumbles through the undergrowth to the soil where it will rest and decay and someday spawn new life and new mystery. It is only with a calm mind and patient feet that I can discover such simple splendor. It is only alone that my eyes and my ears will know it for what it is. It is only the grace of nature that will allow me to find peace with my place in this marvelous world of underestimated phenomenon.

I experienced a unity between my novel and this journal. After writing that previous paragraph here in my red notebook by pencil, I realized there was a place where it fit perfectly into the novel, so I added it by rewriting with the keypad of my laptop. I feel like I am cheating somehow, but they are my words so I can use them where I want. This journal is an outlet to express my honest and simple thoughts, but if something develops here that could be applied to my fiction, I will use it.

Mayana arrived and promptly took off on a voyage with her camera, so I let her spend some time alone with the forest. I decided to begin reading *The Island of Dr. Moreau*, by H.G. Wells. I enjoyed how it questioned the separation between man and beast. Especially this line: "There it must be, I think, in the vast and eternal laws of matter, and not in the daily cares and sins and troubles of men, that whatever is more than animal within us must find its solace and its hope." I spent the afternoon reading and wandering around the woods. This is the best time of year to go sojourning. The humidity has decreased, the mosquitoes and wood ticks have both receded, and the animals are actively preparing for winter.

Sly is taking full advantage of being in the wild. He runs to the river to chase fish, frogs, and turtles, and then returns to camp to hunt every sound in the forest. It is deer hunting season and I frequently hear gunshots, so I put the larger bell on Sly's collar. This makes it more difficult for him to stalk his prey, but he has adapted by walking slower with a smoother gait.

Reading all day makes me lethargic. I'm going to try to stay alert and fish this evening and then have a fire. I think I will get active and cut some firewood.

...

I realized I was in the mind state to write more creatively than journalistically, so I spent some time working on my novel. This was the first time I have written in it while Mayana was at camp, and I felt inspired by reading the words of Wells.

Mayana is asleep in the tent as I sit outside and

listen to owls hooting. For a while, it was the eerie cry of the screech owl. Now it is the repetitive hoot of a barred owl. Earlier there were coyotes singing. Shortly after that, several wolves howled from nearby. Just a few minutes ago, there was a loud snap of a branch from about fifty feet away. The air is calm so it seems unlikely to be a windfall. I will never forget all the sounds in the forest. Tonight is especially loud.

Earlier today while Mayana was on her voyage, I sat beside the river reading, but lost focus while being entertained by a beaver swimming in the water, slapping its tail and meandering within thirty feet of me.

September 10 Saturday

The forest is filled with autumnal activity. Geese are flying overhead, honking their trumpets to gather their community for warmer air. The birds bravely flutter to the forest floor, gathering nuts and seeds. Chipmunks go scurrying past me with cheeks larger than their bellies. The branches of beaked hazel and pin cherry have been picked dry by hyperphagic bears. The buck deer has returned and bugles his mating song into the night. The owls awake before dark to take advantage of the living forest floor before much of it recedes into hibernation. Even the sun is retreating quicker from the cold of night. All but the leaves of trees have accepted their fate, but even they will surrender soon. All it takes is the first frost. It is close. Last night was the first night that I became frigid. There have been other nights when I felt a chill, but last night the air was definitely cold, feeling like it dropped well below fifty degrees. The warmth will only lessen from here.

Today was difficult. I didn't fall asleep until late

last night. I remember waking up in the middle of the night. I was confused by the light on my tent walls. I stared for a while wondering what could be burning so bright. Then I realized it was the sun, it was already morning. I looked over at Mayana who was deep in dreams, so I went back to sleep.

I didn't start working until after 1:00 p.m. I explained to Mayana that it was important for me to work during the weekends so that I could finish before leaving camp for the season. She was okay with this and excited to spend another day with her camera. I added 3,500 new words before dinner.

I am tired so will read myself to sleep. Mayana is already in the tent and has been for a while. She spent most of her weekend wandering through the woods with her camera. I hope she got some good shots for her to view during the coming week while confined to her office desk. I am certain she is great at her job, and I presume she enjoys it, but I look forward to the day I can take her away from that world and share this forest with her full time.

September 11 Sunday

Grouse were drumming in the forest today. I read up on them in the guidebooks and learned that drumming is strictly a springtime activity. I laughed and unlearned that lesson. The most marvelous thing about wild animals is that they tend to break the rules men make for them. Animal behavior cannot be fully defined or predicted any more than human behavior. Each member of the species is a unique experiment of originality.

I cut a large supply of firewood and then prepared a shower. I may have been greedy, wanting a long hot shower, and filled the bucket full to the brim. This was more weight than the rope could support. The result was a broken shower bucket. So I heated up a smaller amount of water and bathed with a sponge. This will be the method I use for the rest of my stay.

September 12 Monday

Occasionally, I do miss the presence of people, but I have gained a greater appreciation for my solitude. I have always enjoyed solitude and had spent many short durations camping alone prior to this adventure. I now realize those trips were nothing but brief interludes, and not enough to fully grasp the power of true isolation. The power surges through stages. First, it is a relief to be alone with nature, and a weight seems to be lessened. The sights, sounds, and smells of these new surroundings are noticed, but the mind is still preoccupied with recent encounters of other people, working out the real meaning of their words and the intentions of their body language. The initial relief is a placebo and the senses are not fully aware because they are distracted by the existence of a separate world. Then comes the realization of being alone, and at first this is good because there is focus; but that focus is still on how different it feels here than in the company of others. Next, the lonesomeness develops; it is a sense of hollowness and wanting for someone to share this experience with. Now the power is emptiness, and this develops fear. Fear is the difficult stage because it is the most logical. A person should be afraid to be alone in the wild because there are many dangers, even in today's tamed forests. There is a reason our species developed into a social one—for security. The fear never really goes away but next comes understanding.

Understanding fear and living with it for many solitary nights transforms it into the bully from school whom I sat next to in class and walked beside in the halls, the one I loathed to see but knew I must learn to tolerate and manage. Punching that bully in the face may have caused him to shy away, but there was still the remembrance of what he was. There was a sense of comfort because the fears felt conquered, and the fight made me feel stronger in his presence. Now the mind has more time to view this new world, and the sights, sounds and smells that had been here all along become heightened by an ability to defend against the fear.

There is comprehension in this isolation. The voices of other people are still heard, but I am now free to hear my own voice. My actions are decided by me alone. I know my place in this world and it is here in the forest.

September 13 Tuesday

I spent the afternoon reading all of Part II from my novel. I was planning to write more, but it's difficult for me to find creativity with all these real life events in my mind. This weekend I will be married.

I spent the evening preparing camp for our wedding party; it's going to be a small group with eight of our siblings and their dates. I cut a large supply of firewood, both at camp and down by the river. I disassembled the three-man dome tent that has been set up at the edge of camp and has been used as overflow storage, and set it up by the river. This will be the newlyweds' room. I also cleaned out the tent Sly has been using as his sanctuary, and this will be used as a guest room; he's going to be disappointed when I don't let him in there during the rest of this week.

September 14 Wednesday

Only two days until I am married, and this thought seems alien to me. I have known many women, but the longest I have ever spent in direct company with one was less than a year that I lived with Mayana prior to this adventure of solitude. I have always wanted to become a family man and to have the opportunity my parents had. I have known Mayana would be my wife for as long as I have known her, but I do not know what kind of husband I will be.

I have an image in my head of being the hard-working provider, of being the man of the house and having children who admire and respect me. I do not know if this is how it will go because the future is unpredictable, and I am a man of many distractions. If I were able to send one message to the future me, it would be, "Love them in real life with the same power you loved them in your dreams." I believe this will come easy for me, but will they love me the same?

Tonight I will leave camp and return to town. In two days I will be married, and I have yet to see our wedding rings or my wedding attire. The future is happening fast and it is time to prepare. I am going to plug in my laptop and write my vows.

...

In the course of drinking a pot of instant coffee, I was able to write my vows. There is so much to say and printed words are never enough. In case I die before the wedding, and my laptop is destroyed but this notebook survives, I will record my wedding vows here in hopes that Mayana would discover them and be pleased:

Like all of the footsteps we take through the dreams that we share,
May we walk side by side.
Like the thousand-million leaves that surround us in gold,
May we shine so bright.
Like the morning birds that sing their rapturous tune,
May we always be so happy.
Like the giant tree that grows a ring every year,
May these rings make us stronger.
Like the great river that flows its eternal course,
May we always know the direction.
Like the paddles that glide gracefully upstream
The rivers of night and the days of dream
All of those tomorrows in the garden at play
The mountains, the meadows, and every single yesterday
The wind and the rain and the snows all may fall
The sun it will shine and the forest will call
Like the back porch dances no eyes ever see
All I want from this life is for you to feel free
Spontaneous adventure whether sunny or grey
Like the hands of a compass I will never lead you astray
I know that you know the words I love you
If you give me your hand I will promise that I do.

I hope she is impressed. I have no idea what to expect from her vows, but I'm certain they will be beautiful.

It is getting late and so time for me to pack up and leave. I will be leaving you at camp, dear journal friend of mine. You have been good to me and deserve to be present for my wedding, but you are at your best while in the wild, and so here you will stay. When I return in several days, I will be a married man and I will be bringing people with me.

September 17 Saturday

The forest trail is tiled with golden leaves. Has it really been so long since I left? I returned this afternoon with the wedding convoy, and they didn't notice the changes in this forest because it was the first they had seen it, but to me it was different. I noticed the bare branches and the weasel tracks through camp. I saw the small animal hole dug into the fire pit, and I knew this only happened because there had been no fire for several days. I recognized my tent, but after being in a city the past few nights, it seemed small, and I wondered what fool would live here. I observed the sun in the sky and it was further south than it had been which meant winter would come soon. I took a moment to soak all of this in before the celebration began.

I was hesitant to bring a wild party to camp because I only know it in its natural silence, and I did not want to alter this image in my mind, but I am now a married man and the party must happen.

We arrived with a trunk full of beer and margarita mix. We filled two coolers with several varieties of beer and played a game called Random Draw; whenever one of us wanted a beer we opened the cooler and grabbed a can without viewing our selection. Whichever one we removed we drank. We smoked fat cigars by the campfire and they tasted like wood and ash. The inhale and exhale was exciting. Blowing smoke rings in the calm forest air was followed by a deep swallow of cheap beer, and this too was exciting. There was no judgment in the wild, and so indulgences were plentiful. There were no regulators here and we were free to indulge in the deep intoxications that made our minds free.

I am alone by the fire now and the last beer is nearly empty. One by one, the party retreated to their tents. Mayana is present, but she sleeps on the ground just behind me. My brother was the last to remain. We ran out of firewood so gathered some in the dark forest. We sat by the bright flames and told stories while flinging our knives and spitting tobacco juice on the hot rocks. My brother put up a good fight, but tonight I outlasted him. I am quite drunk and it is difficult to read my handwriting, but my mind is clear and I love this place after dark.

I look at Mayana curled up and passed out on the earth behind me. We were married September 16 on the shores of Lake Bemidji, with Paul Bunyan as our witness. My wife and I checked into a hotel for the night, and then met up with the wedding convoy earlier this morning for breakfast before driving to camp. It was much fun tonight being with our siblings and telling stories, but I am ready to be alone again. There were many moments in mid-conversation when I stepped away from the circle of chairs and into the silence of the trees. I looked back at them and they didn't belong here, even though I was enjoying their company. I believe the forest prefers to be *unpeopled*.

September 18 Sunday

We were all a mess when we woke up this morning. The fire pit was surrounded by empty beer cans and the embers still smoked. What kind of wild animal had created such a mess?

I helped them pack up and walked them to their cars. Mayana was the last to leave and it was awkward to see her go. We are still the same as we ever were, except now we are married. We will be apart for a couple more weeks and that isn't much time. I will go to bed early and wake up focused to write. I will finish my novel and then move to town and start a new life. There have been many new lives and that is the best part of living.

September 19 Monday

Now I return to solitude. The trees are silent. Presently, I am alone and have packed up most of camp. The nights have been cold, in the thirties, so I will likely only get two or three more weeks here. This is a disheartening case of reality. I decided to start removing items from camp that won't be needed.

It is strange being alone after spending the previous several days in the company of other people. The most awkward part is refraining from the urge to explain what I am doing. When there are other eyes watching, it seems natural to say, "I'm going to cut some firewood," or, "I think I'll walk to the river." In the absence of company, I still think the same thoughts, but there is no one to speak with. I go about my day in silence, and dive further into my own mind. It's amazing to hear my own voice clearly, without a word to be spoken.

September 20 Tuesday

There was a skunk near camp today. I saw it scurry into the fern garden around mid-afternoon, so I kept Sly secured in the tent the rest of today. Something must have spooked or angered it, because the air was laden with the unmistakable odor. At this proximity, it is powerful, like burnt rubber that has been lathered with garlic and rotten tomatoes. It stings my eyes more than the freshest and most potent onion. There is a taste in my mouth similar to tap water with exceedingly high iron concentrations. But there is a positive side; it seems to repel mosquitoes better than citronella. It amazes me that an animal so small and cute can produce such repugnant aroma. Biology works in deceptive ways. The same is true for humans. That thought reminds me of a story, but I will try to be brief because I have nearly filled this notebook, and there are still a couple weeks remaining at camp.

I once had a friend who wasn't really my friend. I remember when he arrived new to our school, and I was drawn to him because he was different. My other friends at the time wanted nothing to do with him for the same reason. There was a rebellious spirit inside of me that had yet to be explored, and this new student provided a gateway. We started getting into trouble with the law, and pretty soon, our reputation invited a group of misfits to join us. We hooked up with a gang from another town and this union made us feel more powerful and righteous in our rebellion. This friend, whose name I will not use, was with me every day, and I did everything I could for him. I thought the favors were reciprocated, so when my car was broken into and my expensive stereo system stolen, I called on him for help.

There was another gang in a nearby town that we had a feud with, a feud that originated over a young woman. My nameless friend convinced me these were the people responsible, so we loaded up a caravan of twenty plus guys and went to their hangout. When we found them, it was a fight and weapons were used. That was the most bloody and bruised I have ever been, but I gave my share as well. The police arrived and arrested us all, at least those of us who were not finished with the fight and so did not run, and I spent the night in a cell with my nameless friend. We felt proud and powerful and knew it would be good for our bad reputation. The fight did not result in the return of my stereo system.

That trend continued to the breaking point, and my parents were fed up with bailing me out of jail. My criminal record grew long, but most of my crimes went undetected. Several years passed — what seemed like an eternity — and I was running in circles around a dead end. A member of our gang had been forced to enter therapy as part of probation, and his life was changing for the better, so the rest of us mocked him for that.

I mocked him for his new clothes and the new music he listened to, until he disclosed some information that shocked me.

He was nearly in tears when he confessed to participating in the theft of my stereo several years back. He had hardly known me at the time so he hadn't felt like it was an assault against a friend. He said it wasn't his idea anyway, but that my nameless friend had suggested it and led them to my house. This was difficult for me to believe because we had been running together for several years. When I confronted him, I could see in his eyes that it was true. I had initiated fights for much less, but with him I felt cheated and this made me more confused than angered, so instead of swinging my fist, I said I was done with him and walked away.

I renounced my criminal ways and have never gone back. A change began and it led me to the forest. I am no longer upset with him because the price of my stereo was well worth the lesson learned, and who knows where I would be today were it not for that event. I would more likely be in prison than here in the wild.

September 21 Wednesday

I wonder how many mosquitoes I have consumed this season. I removed two from my cup of coffee, and thought if they were foolish enough to dive into this hot acidic drink, then surely they have hidden themselves in my food. Actually, the more I think about it, the happier I am to be consuming mosquitoes. The millions of them who live in this forest all want to devour me. I take pride in the few of my enemies I have eaten.

September 22 Thursday

There is much of this world I haven't seen, and much

of what I have has disappointed me. But there are many sights so remarkable that their image remains clear in my vision long after they have passed from view. I have seen waterfalls pouring off the face of a mountain. I have seen newborn moose calves frolicking in a wild stream. I have seen the tracks of cougars in fresh snow. I have seen the sun rise over the ocean, and in every direction only water. I have watched the nymph of a dragonfly crawl onto shore and shed its skin to reveal a most remarkable specimen of flight. And I have seen a beautiful woman walking through the woods with a crate of ice, a bag of food, and a bottle of vodka. My Wife arrived today for an extra-long weekend, and that is all I have time to say.

September 23 Friday

Mayana brought me a newspaper. I have been completely disconnected from current events, and it has been good to ignore the headlines that have no effect on my life. This article had an immediate effect on my life, and she didn't give it to me last night because she didn't want me to be upset on our first evening reunited as husband and wife. It was about Minnesota adopting a wolf-hunting season.

I thought of the first time I ever encountered a wolf. I was hiking alone down a backcountry trail northeast of Ely, MN. It was a sunny day and I walked towards the Kawishiwi River. He came out of the forest and paused 100 feet ahead of me and cocked his head in my direction. I stood entirely still and waited for him to make a move. His eyes were wild, and his posture was that of a creature always free. I made a movement to set my pack on the ground, and the wolf shuffled into the thick brush and was immediately out of sight.

I continued down the trail and setup camp beside the river. That night I heard a single wolf howling and I imagined it was him. The sound of a howling wolf may be the greatest sound on Earth.

I think back on that animal now with great fondness. To the supporters of this wolf hunt I say shoot him if you must, he will die free and that is better than most. You will die unfulfilled and never be free. You will not be greatened by taking his life. His life will always be great and death will not steal that. There is no stealing the wilderness, and what was made here will always be so. You cannot remove it for it will return without your permission. If you are lost then time spent in the wild will be better than attempting to kill it. If you do not fear the wilderness there will be no reason to fight it. If you are strong and secure then there is nothing left to kill, and you will respect that which is also strong and secure. The trees, water, and wolf were here before you, and they know their place in the cycle. Man is young in this land, and our place in the cycle is being determined every day. The choices we make and the actions we take will determine if we as a species make the land better, or are ultimately responsible for its demise.

When I hear the wolves howl, it solidifies my sense of wilderness. I have heard them one of every four nights while at camp. I lived in the wild state of Wyoming and had a great job, but the wolf was what brought me back to Minnesota. I hope they live in this place forever. If this forest lost its wolf, this land would lose its value to me.

September 24 Saturday

What I fear most now is not the darkness or the possible dangers in the forest. What I fear now is my return to civilization. What I fear is interacting with people, and knowing they won't understand. What I fear is knowing they are unhappy with their lives but don't know what to do about it.

I don't want to see people burdened by responsibilities they don't believe in. I don't want to see people unaware of their potential because they have never had the opportunity to explore it. I don't want to retreat to the use of possessions as a surrogate for my happiness. I don't want to want anything.

September 25 Sunday

Autumn is receding into winter, and I am a full participant. Last night it was dark by seven p.m. I could see my breath inside the tent, even with the body heat from Mayana and two dogs. I had plenty of sleeping bags, my clothes were layered, and I wore a stocking cap and gloves. I didn't feel cold, even when the temperature continued to drop overnight.

···

We had a great Sunday, again. We slept late, and then my Wife made a large breakfast. After eating, we sat by the river and sipped coffee before taking a long canoe ride this afternoon. The leaves change more every day. Today the river was vibrant with the autumnal colors of orange, red and yellow.

My Wife left early this evening, and Canyon, her dog, is staying at camp for the week. I spent the remainder of daylight packing up camp and loading the trailer. This is distracting from creativity, the thought that my time here is almost over, and I wonder if I've done enough. Can I finish what I intended to in the short remainder of fair weather? My novel lives here in the forest with me. When I finish the story and take it away, it will be as though I am removing a component of this ecosystem.

The wolves sing loudly tonight, and I will fall asleep while listening to their songs of the wild.

September 26 Monday

It was the type of day that can only exist in the forest. I woke up early and walked to the river. The forest was misty and damp from the cold air of night. I entered the tent and returned to bed. I slept fairly late, because it was a cold morning and I was more comfortable beneath the sleeping bags. Last night I stayed up listening to music and wrote on the laptop. This was fun, but the use was too much and drained my solar battery. This morning it was too low to use, so I carried it up to exchange with the fully charged one in my Jeep. This is great leg exercise; if I did it once a day, I would be in prime hockey condition.

I settled into writing early this afternoon. It took a lot of coffee to get me going. I reread all of Part II and then added 1,200 new words. It's difficult to get in the groove of creativity with so many real life thoughts in my mind. My goal is to finish this week. I need to wrap it up; it's getting so long that each part could be split into its own book. Once I get going, I fall into another world quite easily. Sometimes it seems like the imagined world is the one actually happening. I know it's going well when reality fades from perception.

I called my Wife tonight. She sounded excited as we discussed plans for our honeymoon to Florida. This will be the first time I meet her father and brother.

I want to turn on my computer, listen to loud music,

and read through my writings, maybe even look at pictures. I must restrain myself. I cannot drain another battery, it is the only one I have for the week. If it goes dry, I will be forced to go home and charge it. It seems that whatever temptations are available, no matter how small, they pull at me with magnificent force. It is a constant battle to fight against them. The temptations usually win.

I spent the early hours of night beside the river. It was cloudy and mostly dark so the river looked black and soft. There was much noise in the forest, and I heard a large fish splash in the river. It is simple to be alone, and offered me much time to think.

Eventually, I wandered back to the tent, and the trail was barely illuminated by the moon burning through the clouds. I lit a couple candles to read for a while before making this entry. There are many thoughts that seem to scatter, and I want to grasp as many as I can.

I have learned many lessons alone in the woods, but most of them indefinable, and only exist the way a life exists—too vast and complex to be described. One of them can be summarized by saying: I value love, and someday I hope to have a child, so that I may love somebody the way my parents loved me. That would be the type of love truly unconditional, because even if my child grew to despise me, my love would never change. I hope to get that opportunity, and with Mayana, I believe I will.

Forgive me journal, I have fallen into the sentimental again. This was not my intention, but it is inevitable while alone for me to long for someone else. The longing is not so bad, except it makes me feel hollow. The hollowness was not so easy at first, because in the woods there was nothing to fill it, but then I realized that darkness was hollow also, and if I blew out the candles we would be hollow together. Nothing can be hollow in company.

September 27 Tuesday

There is electricity at camp. It is bright and vibrant and blinding. It crackles and dances and moves too fast to follow. There is more lightning in the sky than I have ever seen.

The storm clouds travel slowly on a south wind and are high in the sky. The most powerful storms always seem to move slowly. The air is heavy with humidity and so stale that it is difficult to breathe. I sit outside in my boxers and tank top, and the mosquitoes are ferocious. The tops of the trees bend and sway, and when the storm comes, some of them will fall.

I enjoy the mystery of the storm and watching it move, but there is something terrifying about being here alone with it. Tornadoes are rare this far north, but rare does not mean impossible, and when they occur, they are generally malevolent. The lightning alone could kill me, but at least it produces a great show.

I hear it coming like an avalanche, but I will not run. I can only dig in. If this is my final entry, dear journal friend, let any eyes who ever read you know that I died happy.

September 28 Wednesday

I was kept awake by the storm and did not sleep much. The electricity and wind were both strong, but the rain was minimal. It is early morning and the new sun reaches through the trees. The sunlight is crisp and flows in perfect lines.

One of the taller aspen trees within camp fell to

the ground twenty feet from my tent. I walked the trail from the Jeep to the river and saw many others that had fallen as well. The night was loud and the ground shook. I wonder how the wolves fared.

I brewed some instant coffee and then cut the fallen aspen into sizes I could roll out of camp. I plugged in my solar equipment and then sat down to write. Feeling as though I had just survived a near-death experience, I was highly inspired and had a productive day, adding 6,700 new words. When I finished writing and sat down to read *Of Time and Place*, by Sigurd F. Olson, I realized that I had a new respect for authors, and that I read much differently now that I have gotten so far with this project. I imagine the writer equally, if not more, than the characters. So much of a person's life goes into a story, albeit a refined and disordered version. Makes me realize how many events happen in every single life that can be dramatized into enjoyable fiction.

There was a mild shower of golden leaves today as the autumn breeze blew them from trees. I enjoy standing beneath a colony of aspen trees and looking up at the golden silhouettes flickering in the sunlight and drifting down. This created a mysterious image, as if the sky were crumbling into golden flakes. With the reduction of leaves and the undergrowth receding, I can see further into the forest. This I enjoy, but I know soon it will become a winter landscape, and I will not be here to view it.

I went fishing this evening and cast large flies for muskie. The water was more turbid than usual from the debris blown in by last night's storm. No catch. I only fished for half an hour because I could hear the dogs howling and growling over a mile away. Hopefully I can get my Wife to keep both the dogs in town for a week before the season ends, so I can get some real fishing in.

September 29 Thursday

I am mentally famished. I worked on Part III today. I wrote 9,800 words. That is all I have left to say on the subject.

I have given up hope for catching a muskie this season, but I would like to catch at least one fish. Tomorrow I will paddle to the rapids and cast for smallmouth bass.

I spent much of the day calling for the dogs. They kept pushing each other further and further from camp. I saw Canyon chasing an agitated woodpecker from tree to tree. Then he spooked up a grouse. Later he followed a squirrel as it evaded him in the treetops.

It was raining golden leaves most of the day. Soon the trees will be bald. I tried to take pictures of falling leaves, but I have a rudimentary camera and the shutter speed was too slow.

Between writing my book, writing this journal, taking photographs, identifying plants and birds, taking nature walks, fishing, canoeing, and kayaking, this has been the summer of my dreams. How could it get any better? I have a beautiful woman (now my Wife) who arrives for conjugal visits every weekend with supplies. Perhaps I am dead. This is the closest thing to heaven a man like me could ever know.

September 30 Friday

There were high winds most of the day, and they tore the anchor ropes from the tarp that was over my sanctuary. With so little time remaining at camp, I decided not to fix it, but rather folded it up and placed it in the trailer.

I spent some time lying in the hammock by the river. On my way down, Sly spooked up a grouse and took off after it. As I was lying in the hammock daydreaming, an American kestrel landed in the dead ash tree nearby. These are magnificently colored falcons, the first one I have seen here. Later, while I was in the screen house with Sly taking a nap beside me, a grouse approached. I watched him get within ten feet of us before Sly awoke and gave chase. I spent the evening sitting outside deep in thought. I am trying to create the next part of my story, but my thoughts are mostly pragmatic about the end of my season here in the wild. It's not over yet. I need to utilize these real life ideas for imaginary purpose. Transform the truth into fiction.

I saw two piles of fresh wolf scat on the driveway today.

October 1 Saturday

Mayana arrived late last night, and we decided to sleep in the tent that was still set up by the river from our wedding party. We had a fire beneath the arms of Bartholomew, and the air was calm, so the smoke clung to the cedar palms. A thick layer of mist dangled above the river this morning as we crawled from the tent. I was hungry and wanted to walk up to camp to eat, but this sight was too magnificent to leave, so we sat on the shore until the morning sun burned away the mist.

October 2 Sunday

This will likely be my final week at camp. Mayana is

aware of this fact and offered to spend the day canoeing so I could write. I think this was a polite way for her to spend the day canoeing. That's great because I want her to experience some of the solitude I have felt. I know that nobody in my life will ever understand what it was for me to spend four months alone in the wild, but I want Mayana to feel it. This is not for the sake of sympathy or empathy, but because she deserves the sensation.

While she was with the river, I wrote 10,400 words. If I were in a foreign city, I would walk down a cobblestone street and announce it to the world. Instead, I walked to the river, and every tree, bush, and animal track made sense. The world was illuminated with definition, and I felt able to grasp the illusive nature of my surroundings. After sitting beside the river and drinking a celebratory beer, I walked back to camp and wrote another 450 words. These words included the final sentence. My novel is complete, though it is far from finished.

When Mayana returned from the river, she cooked dinner and we sat beside the fire. It got dark early and she went to bed, but my thoughts were too scattered, so I gathered more wood. I thought finishing my novel would be a relief, but mostly I am wanting more. There are many thoughts remaining that I haven't found a place for. A part of my mind is missing and that is because I gave it to the novel. It is difficult for me to imagine a stranger reading my mind, because we are all so critical about our differences. I want my novel to be known and to reach as many people as possible, but I want to be hidden. I want to be anonymous, because if they know me there will be certain expectations, and I don't think they would understand.

October 3 Monday

It's difficult for me to express how it feels to be completely alone in this absolute darkness. I did not have a fire tonight, and the sky is cloudy, so not even the stars or moon are visible. Every space around my periphery is black, and the places behind my periphery are even darker. This world that exists without light is heavy. It compresses and squeezes me and then pulls me apart. Every blank spot in my view is a threat, and the places where a faint light illuminates a mysterious shape are even more dangerous because there the mind has an inkling of definition to exaggerate from. The exaggerations are the hard part, and the most difficult to control. There is an instinct buried in my subconscious that desires a conflict, a midnight marauder, a beast ready to feast upon me. So I absorb it. I stick the blade of my knife into the ground beside my feet and I say let them come. The other half of my brain says nothing will come, that I am being paranoid and ridiculous, but that half is easily muted by the volume of darkness.

Presently I sit at the writing desk in my tent, and there is a single-wick candle burning beside me. I must lean close to the pages and squint my eyes to read what I am writing. I look out from the screen window but see absolutely nothing. Inside, the candle light flickers on the canvas walls, and the shadows move fast in obscure shapes. There is not much light, but it is enough to distinguish from darkness. The light feels safe even though it tells me nothing more than what I already know—I am surrounded by a world so incomprehensible that no amount of light could ever define it.

I get up to take a piss in the milk carton, and it is cold so I shiver, it is dark so I cannot see, it is quiet but I hear an animal crawling outside. I am alone, but I am free. It is only alone that any man can ever be free. I seal the milk carton and crawl into bed. I am cold and I shiver even though the blankets are thick above me. It is dark and I see nothing, but my imagination is full. This is the darkest darkness and most silent silence I have ever known.

October 4 Tuesday

My novel is complete, and both the dogs are in town with Mayana. This is my final week, and I am alone with a river. There are fish in the river, and it's time they share my company.

I waded barefoot in shorts and a long sleeve shirt. A cool day with blue skies and soft white clouds. The sound of my fly line cutting through the air, and the water cutting around me. The tug of a fish and the joy of a fight.

I was half a mile upstream when the fish struck. I cast a large streamer pattern into the middle of a riffle and let it drift down into the deep pool below. I stood on the right edge of water and stripped in line. The pull was solid and unmistakably from a large fish.

I set the hook hard and held my line until the fish forced it downstream. I followed along in the shallows and kept my rod tip high to prevent the fish from holding to the bottom. It felt strong and heavy, but also dead, like the weight of a submersed log. I pulled as hard as I could without breaking the knot, but the fish would not rise. I thought the fish had ditched my hook and left it snagged on a boulder until my line started to move. When I saw its head break through the surface, I knew it was too large to be landed. It looked like the trunk of a tree that had been stripped of its bark. My heart pounded fast with the adrenaline of combat. I was both terrified and excited.

As I pulled on my line, I realized this caused me to move towards the fish more than the fish towards me. I began wading downstream while pulling the line gently, hoping the fish would turn. There was a shallow spot near my shoreline where I could wade out further and make a good fight. The fish wouldn't budge, and I could see it bobbing up and down on the surface with a body easily over forty inches long. I was going to land it but didn't know how.

I circled upstream so I could pull it into the current, hoping to tire the fish out. Pulling against the current made the fish heavier and gave it more leverage to fight. My rod was flexed like a U when the leader broke. All it took was one violent splash of the tail and the fish was free of me. I watched its head bob up one more time and then disappear beneath the surface, and my heart ached.

I sat on the shore for a while before I made peace

with my loss. It had been a good fight, and that was the largest fish I had ever hooked. The knowledge of such a powerful opponent inspired me to fish more. This winter I will tie flies, and next summer the sun will shine, my knots will be strong, and my leader will not give. I am allowing you one more season to enjoy this victory, muskie, and then it will be mine.

October 5 Wednesday

I have reduced camp to only what is required for the next several nights. I have disassembled the spare tents and sanctuary. I have packed up most tools and fishing gear. Today I will load whatever will fit in the Jeep and drive to town. I will stay there one night with Mayana and then return to camp tomorrow. This will be a short entry because I am not happy about leaving and don't have much more to say.

October 6 Thursday

I decided to stay in town an extra night so I could play hockey. It has been too long and I have thought about it much. I am not finished with the forest, but it is time to make peace with my inevitable departure.

It is awkward making a journal entry in this house; these walls are less conducive to clear thoughts than the trees. Plus, there's not much to write about — life is quite boring in town. I did have pizza today, and that was spectacular. Not much else occurred other than drinking better coffee and listening to music without the threat of draining a battery.

But then there was hockey. Hockey is the greatest sport because it requires physical prowess and creative application, all in split-second increments. I arrived to the rink with a long beard and wild hair, certainly not the first hockey player to fit this description. Yet I must have looked different, or perhaps the smell of the forest was with me, because several of the players commented on me looking like a recluse.

Thinking back on it now, I'm sure their intentions were good, and they were only stating observations, but at the time, I took it as an offense and refused to be judged by these domesticated strangers. I got riled up and nearly started a fight on the ice. This may be common practice in professional games, but it is rare to see at recreational games when everyone playing has to get up and look presentable for work the following day. I had nobody to look presentable for tomorrow, but in this, I was alone. It's a shame that to fit in and be respected requires the numbing of our instincts.

I felt alien and estranged after the game when all of the guys were engaged in conversations. I had nothing to say and just wanted to be back in the forest. I realized then that nature has ruined me for other people, and I smiled.

October 7 Friday

Sly and I returned to camp for the final night this season. I am happy to be home, but I am also sad to be leaving. Sadness is a direct correlation to the happiness previously felt, so I must have been extremely happy. I remember the forest on my first day here, and I will never forget being part of its changes. They say we can take nothing when we die, but we can leave something of ourselves behind. I wonder what the forest will remember of me, and my brief application on this landscape.

It is cloudy and cool and looks like snow. A cold wind blows through the trees and I watch an aspen leaf meander to the ground. It shimmers and shakes and takes its time. In the forest, there is never a rush because each season has its purpose and reason. I wait for the leaf to land and then walk over and pick it up. It grew as I grew, changed as I changed, and now we leave together, departed from these trees but forever connected to this place.

October 8 Saturday

I am sitting by the river listening to the wind and watching the grey water slide by. Soon I will return to the city and this season will be a memory. Tomorrow my life will change, but this river will still flow and these trees will remain. I will return, but when I do, the forest will not recognize me. There is an affinity between mankind and the wild, but it is not earned fast or easy. You must put in your time and sharpen your focus, or your mind will forever be confined to the luxuries of the city, your spirit will be dampened by the requirement of conformity, and you will never know the power of solitude.

...

It is getting late and I must leave. I broke camp and loaded the trailer this morning, and have been sitting by the river since. Sly is with me, and he spent much of the day fishing, but he had the same success rate as I had all summer. He has worn himself out and sits beside me.

There was a rustling of leaves on the forest floor across the river. Sound travels further this time of year. I could hear the footsteps long before I knew what made them. Sly heard them too and perked up his ears and watched. When the wolf came out of the forest on the opposite side of the river, neither Sly nor I made a move. He got near the river's edge before he sensed us. He stopped in his tracks and held his position. He seemed more curious than afraid. I noticed that he and Sly were making eye contact, studying each other. It may have been my imagination, but I sensed a recognition of deep and profound kinship between the two as they admired the other from across the river. I know this is a worn out metaphor, but in that moment, this river represented a separation of time — the wild and free wolf on one side, with the domesticated and trained dog on the other. Two members of the same species and similar appearance, separated by this endless current of change, divided by time and circumstance.

I was amazed by how long the two watched each other without making a move. I imagined a silent conversation happening between them. The wolf looking at Sly and saying, "You have been wild, now you understand." Sly looking at the wolf and answering, "Yes, I have been wild, but you have never been civilized. I hope you never understand."

After the wolf had enough, he wagged his tail slightly, and then, with the same leisure with which he arrived, departed back into the trees. I think we interrupted his visit to the drinking hole. After all of the signs and late night howls I have encountered this season, that was the only wolf to make contact. I am glad Sly got to see him with me.

It started raining hard immediately after the wolf vanished, so I rushed to the trailer and secured a tarp over my supplies. It has rained for the past two hours. I sit alone in what used to be my camp, covering my notebook with the hood of my raincoat, and I can see my breath in the cold air. I should have left hours ago, and Mayana is likely worried, but I am not ready.

I am struggling more than ever to put my thoughts into words. I would like to live like this forever. I wonder how I will adapt to city life. My greatest hope is to forever retain the serenity of mind that was earned in the forest. Now I must travel out, back into the world of men, into the world of machines, into the world of destruction. I will do my best to forget what I learned here, because the rules of the forest do not apply to the life in a city.

Goodbye trees. Goodbye neighbors. Goodbye river. Next time we meet will be a time for blooms. Please don't change too much…

Ten Years Later...

Beartooth Mountains, MT, 2021

Take a step outside and take a look around
right at yourself
I wonder what you found.

Jan. 14, 2021

I arrived at a Forest Service cabin in the Beartooth Mountains of Montana earlier this evening. I will be staying here two nights and am alone but for the exception of my dog, Summit, who is a tail-wagging lapdog of Beagle-Corgi mix. Though he is much different in character than his predecessor, Sly, from ten years prior, I enjoy his company. It is good to have a dog as company, if only to see another pair of eyes and to have another set of ears present so when I speak audibly I'm not talking to myself.

My first task after arriving was to unload the camp supplies. Supplies for two nights in a cabin are quite minimal, and consist of: two sleeping bags, cooking utensils, water filter and thermos, coffee, chamomile tea, brats, Clif bars, beef jerky, Bowie knife, matches, lantern and headlamp, mouthwash, this laptop, plus twenty-seven books. My next task was to start a fire in the wood stove. The Jeep has a thermometer and it read 26 degrees Fahrenheit when I arrived at 4:30 p.m., so it will be a cold couple of evenings. This cabin has electricity so I am writing with my laptop which is plugged into the wall socket. On my desk beside this laptop is the red covered notebook in which I wrote *The Unpeopled Season* ten years ago. I reread it earlier this week and felt transported back to that time and place.

They say memory is selective, but I believe it is more fluid, and changes shape similar to how a river will each season. Its transparency and turbulence, even the design of its course, will fluctuate, but it still begins and ends at the same place. My point is, this is what I realized while rereading the journal: even though years have passed, rarely a day has gone by that I did not think about my time in the forest. The sight of bunchberries sprouting fruit along my trail to camp. The ferns that grew higher than my waist in the course of a summer. The sound of a dried balsam fir as I cracked it beneath my boot into small pieces for the fire. The touch of the river as it glided gracefully downstream. Listening to my rain barrels fill with fresh water dripping from the canvas awning. Tracks of deer and bear and smaller mammals in the soft soil after a rain. The sight of an eagle gliding in calm air and the sound of wolves howling after dark. And yes, I also think fondly of the loneliness, because it was painful, but a variation of pain that brought me pleasure because it encouraged me to look deeper within.

It's been a busy ten years since that summer in the forest. In the spring of 2013 I opened an ice cream shop in Bemidji, MN called Big River Scoop, which was located directly across the street from the Paul Bunyan & Babe the Blue Ox statues under which I married Mayana. Big River Scoop was not your typical ice cream shop — we sold twenty-four flavors, but also made pizza and pasties from scratch, had a small fly fishing shop in the front, and a back area we called The Philosophy Room where you could purchase new and used books. We had wooden Octoberfest benches imported from Germany beside the bay windows where you could sit and look out at the lake. It quickly became a staple to downtown Bemidji — both for residents and tourists — and I realized something had changed. I had become part of a community.

That same spring of 2013 our daughter was born. When she was two weeks of age I brought her camping for the first time at Bemidji State Park, and while she was lying in a meadow beneath tall pines and I was reading nearby, a Franklin squirrel came up and sniffed the top of her head. Mayana was still working as the Director of Planning for the Greater Bemidji Area, and I was busy running a new business, so we did not do much camping. During the next two years, I can count the number of times we visited the forest on one hand. Running a small business had created a rift in our relationship with the land.

In 2014 I self-published the novel I wrote in the forest, *This of a Wilderness*. It was easy for readers to recognize that work as semi-autobiographical, and many of them reached out to me to ask how much of it was true.

So later that year I published this journal, to accompany the novel as its honest twin of sorts. Shortly after, while at a book reading event, I was approached by another writer who said he had written a manuscript about the natural world, and asked me to help publish his book, which I did. This led to another book, and another, and the founding of Riverfeet Press. Since then I have worked on sixteen books about wildlife, adventure and the environment. Publishing as a business is a tricky industry because the market is overly saturated, and many good books go unnoticed for the simple fact they lack a large marketing budget. Yet, I enjoy it very much. It is an opportunity to truly get to know a book from cover to cover, and the author. Plus, I believe it is important to share stories about these themes of wildlife, wilderness and the environment so that we as a civilization don't forget how important wild places are for us.

In the spring of 2016 we sold that piece of land where I lived during the summer of 2011, and Mayana moved west to Montana where she had a job with the Planning Department in Bozeman. Our daughter and I remained in Bemidji to sell the business and the house, and then met her in Montana later that summer. The mountains, trout streams and wide open spaces had been calling us back west ever since we left Wyoming. Yet, I miss that land in northern Minnesota, and even though I sold the deed, I never owned the land. The land owned me. We pay for the right to belong to it. I was lucky to be owned by a good piece of land.

Prior to leaving Minnesota, Sly passed away at the age of sixteen, which, I'm told, is an old age for a Siberian Husky. Dogs are loyal and joyous companions, and I feel I succeeded as his companion by bringing him into wild places where he could run and chase and sniff and dig how he pleased. On an April afternoon I brought him to the property and buried him downhill from camp beside the small creek. There was still snow on the ground and the soil was frozen so it took several hours to dig his grave with my axe and shovel. I placed a copy of the first printing of *The Unpeopled Season* beside his body and covered the top with clinker rocks brought back from Wyoming. Then I knelt in the snow with tears in my eyes and remembered how great it was to see his smile in the wild. I knew it was better that he died before moving to Montana because he belonged to this forest. Whether he remained buried and decomposed into the soil, or was dug up by a wolf or bear, either way his spirit and flesh remain there, and, if I'm lucky, someday I will be buried in a similar fashion.

My first year in Montana was spent exploring the mountains and standing in trout streams. Many nights we camped, and in the process, we discovered new favorite locations. We bought a small house in Livingston, and in the spring of 2017 I opened an outdoor provisions store called Jumping Off Point. This wasn't your typical outdoor store, as we carried a lineup of our custom designed shirts, the essential gear for camping, a selection of books, local meats and cheeses, plus a wide selection of imported beer. As you know from reading this journal, it is my opinion that a beer goes good with a campfire.

In 2018 we opened another business, Farmgirl Pizzeria & Bakery. Each of these shops were voted best new business in our county back-to-back years. That same year a book I published won the Montana Book Award and the High Plains Book Award. All of the sudden life became exceedingly busy. Busy is good if you're focused on success, but the result was we found less time to be in the mountains. So that summer we committed ourselves to a plan we called *Twenty-four Hours a Week*. What this meant was, that no matter how busy or stressed we became, we would spend a minimum of twenty-four hours each week in wild places. This typically involved one long hike in the mountains mid-week, and then an overnight camping trip on Sunday nights. The thing about running a business (or three) is that it's sort of like having a child. The first few years it needs a lot of attention. So our camping trips typically started around 6 p.m. on Sunday nights, and ended at 7 a.m. Monday mornings. These brief interludes with the natural world helped, not only our adult psyches, but the formation of our child's. Still, twenty-four hours a week wasn't enough. We again found ourselves living different than how we intended.

In 2019 we sold the assets for Jumping Off Point and Farmgirl, and then we each went back to working regular jobs, with the idea that this would provide us more free time to spend out-of-doors. Mayana was hired as the Assistant Director of Planning for Gallatin County, and I took a part-time job working several days a week so I could homeschool our daughter and focus on growing Riverfeet Press. We bought a house in the country near the foothills of the Beartooth mountains with a view of Paradise Valley where the Yellowstone River flows north from the park. If I stand on my front porch and look down the valley, I can see canyons cutting into the mountains, and most of them I have explored while hiking, camping and fishing. I remember living in the forest that summer of 2011, and how it was the first place I ever truly felt at home. This was the second.

Here at the cabin it is dark outside and I keep the ceiling lights off inside because I prefer the ambience of a popup lantern — the way it casts shadows across the room. Behind the cabin is a small creek and I can hear it gurgling under the ice. During the warm months this has become my favorite place to cast flies for cutthroat trout, and I've had much better success with these fish than the muskies of my northcountry camp. In the winter it is quiet here, and the nearest human resident this time of year is roughly seven miles to my northwest. So I step outside to listen.

The sound of ice shifting on the frozen river in the middle of night is how I imagine it sounds to drop a sedan from 20 feet. It was certainly loud enough to startle me as I stood in the frigid air. All has gone quiet now, and even though I know it is unlikely any creatures are stirring about, because the bears are hibernating and most mammals have traveled to lower elevations, I still imagine their eyes on me, as my shadow from the lantern spreads across the trees and down to the water. There is something about presenting myself with unrealistic fears that makes me feel alive. It heightens my senses, and then I think, if we aren't occasionally afraid to die, we won't have the context to value living.

Back in the cabin now and I listen to Mozart on my laptop. I will read myself to sleep from the pages of *The Wild Boy* by Paolo Cognetti. Goodnight, dear journal friend. I have missed your company.

Jan. 15, 2021

I step out of the cabin to a calm and sunny morning. There is roughly three inches of snow on the ground which is exceptionally light for this time of year. Inside a fire is burning and I'm heating a cup of instant coffee on top of the wood stove. When it is ready, I pull the camp chair onto the back porch and sit watching steam rise from my coffee cup. The shape of the creek has changed from ice shifting overnight, and from my vantage point I now see an open pool of crystal-clear water with parti-colored cobblestones underneath.

Across the creek is a campground that is closed this time of year. I've brought my family here a cou-ple times each summer, and as I sit on this cabin porch alone, I think back two years ago to the time my daugh-ter practiced using a slingshot while Mayana sat in a camp chair reading and I was thigh-deep in the water casting dry flies to rising trout. I remember realizing that solitude wasn't required to enjoy time in the for-est, and how lucky I was to share that experience with people I loved.

My attraction to wild places is, in part, an attempt to relive the innocence and imagination lost after youth. To be submersed in the innocence of a forest, the un-governed landscape, to exist by my own laws and no one else's, even if only briefly — this is one of the pri-mary beacons that guides me back into wild places. I feel as though with each visit I am searching for some-thing. The intangible comprehension is what I seek, and I come closest to understanding while alone with the trees.

I finished that book, *The Wild Boy*, last night — it was a short read of 162 pages. If you enjoyed reading this journal of mine, I suspect you would also enjoy Cognetti's book about solitude. My favorite line was, "(Mario) spent long, famished days designing a moun-tain cabin. He imagined it in a clearing where he would live by hunting, in solitude, with books for company, in order to cure himself of the war." We all have our own wars to cure ourselves from, and I can think of no better place for this type of convalescence than in wild places.

On any given day in my city life, whether it be a Tuesday or Sunday, there are more assignments on my to-do list than could be finished in a single day, and these become compounded with every passing day. This is considered a good thing because it is a sign of progress, that there is growth and contributions to be made. But it strips me of my natural condition, which is to say, removes part of what is in my source-blood. It is something that is in the source-blood of all of us. That is to feel the world in its primitive form and be grounded by those sensations.

What I find most discomforting about city life — even in a small rural town — is how we must constantly suppress our natural thoughts, push them away, and fill our minds with something much more artificial. It's likely we can go hours, days, even weeks without realizing we are hiding our own true thoughts from ourselves. Then something might happen, and it could be small, easily unnoticed, but this time we notice an event as simple as the robin dipping down from an apple tree, a deer crossing a meadow, or a sheet of snow sliding off of a boulder, and then we begin to remember. We remember that our thoughts are not designed for this mechanical world. No matter how hard we try to succeed at acquiring more manmade objects, or how high we climb up the proverbial ladder, we know, beneath all that, something is missing. And that something is quietude. I can only tell you what I know for certain, and that is we are missing the silence surrounding a frozen river or a leaf tumbling towards the ground.

Silence is the only place where we can actually hear anything. It is important that we discover this silence so we can listen.

I must admit, it is a bit difficult for me today to find that silence, as there are many other thoughts in my head — thoughts, I suspect, that are currently dominating the minds of many Americans. We are in the midst of the Covid-19 pandemic, the president has just been impeached for the second time during his four-year term, and it's been eight days since protesters stormed the Capitol in an attempt to overthrow the election results. So I think back to the summer of 2011 when I was oblivious to the happenings of headlines. I recall writing a line that summer, "For all I know the president could be dead, or worse, Bob Dylan." I typically do not agree with the old adage that ignorance is bliss, because how can we be happy if unaware, but there are certainly exceptions, and being in the forest consumed with its cycles, while ignorant of what is happening in the manmade world, is one of them.

It is extremely difficult to break the habit of checking emails or social media at every pause in activity, and even though there is no internet here, I find myself naturally clicking on the Microsoft Edge icon between each paragraph. So I add a couple logs to the stove and walk down to the creek to filter some water. It is crystal clear and icy cold, and tastes better than any tap I've drank from. A pine squirrel hurries up a tree and a raven squawks above me. The river sounds like chimes as it jangles under the ice and gurgles up from the open spaces. These sights and sounds are so serene, yet my first instinct is to take a picture and post it on social media. Five years consumed with a digital life is a tough drug to ween oneself from. So I walk back into the cabin and pull a chair next to the stove. Here I will sit and read *Hawks Rest*, by Gary Ferguson. A good book is the best cure I know.

...

I just returned from a short hike through the wintry mountains, and several times as Summit ran off ahead of me, I whistled and called out to him, "Come here Sly." It's the first time I've ever called him that.

It's now been twenty-four hours since I saw my wife and daughter. Solitude was much easier as a single man. Now I feel a little more empty than before. I wonder how their day was. Did my daughter get her school work finished? What pictures has she been drawing? Did my wife feel stressed working from home while watching our daughter? Did she miss me? So I stand up and pace the room while drawing pictures of them in my mind.

I step outside into the darkness and snow is falling. Roughly an inch has accumulated on the hood of my Jeep. If it gains intensity and continues through the night, it will be an interesting drive out of here tomorrow. I consider packing up and leaving now, in case a blizzard traps me here, but that won't accomplish anything. I have enough food, water and firewood for several days. Add a couple logs to the fire and turn on my headlamp. The bed is ready for me and I have a book to read.

I lay here in bed trying to focus on the pages of *Hawks Rest*, but I continue to find myself staring off into the darkness thinking about how the ferns at my camp smelled after a rain.

Jan. 16, 2021

It is easy to wake up at sunrise when sleeping in the mountains. I stoke the fire and set a cup of instant coffee on top of the stove. Roll up my sleeping bags and shove them into the Duluth pack. I open the back door and inhale deeply. Winter air at 7,000 feet is crisp and clean, makes the lungs feel whole, and I can smell the pine trees and fresh snow. There is only several inches of new snow, and it is soft, so the drive will be easy.

Over the course of these past ten years, when life gets challenging or stressful, I find a place where I can be alone, even if only for a moment, and I think back to my summer in the forest. There was a section along the shore where I spent a lot of time looking at the river through the branches of a maple tree. I recall images of the trail that I knew so well I could walk it in the dark without tripping on logs or stepping into the badger holes. Each morning I'd awake and see dew glistening on the ferns. As much time as I've spent in wild places and recollections of them, I still feel as though I lack the explanation for why it provides such calm. The nearest I've come was with a line from this journal, "I realized that no words by the tongue of man can express the simplicities of a quiet land, so I returned to the river." And I have continued returning to rivers ever since. As often as possible.

photo by John LaTourelle

Daniel J. Rice was born in Wiesbaden, Germany, in 1979. In 2006 he earned a degree in Watershed Science, in Ely, MN, and began working as a Hydrographer for the U.S. Geological Survey, first in New Jersey, and then Wyoming. In 2011 he resigned from his position and moved alone into a tent deep in the forests of northern Minnesota. He is the founder of five independently owned businesses, including Riverfeet Press. Currently he lives in Livingston, MT, where he spends his time camping and fishing the Beartooth Mountains with his wife and daughter.

For more information and updates, visit:
www.riverfeetpress.com

Other titles from Riverfeet Press

THIS SIDE OF A WILDERNESS: A Novel — Daniel J. Rice

ECOLOGICAL IDENTITY: Finding Your Place in a Biological World
— Timothy Goodwin

ROAD TO PONEMAH: The Teachings of Larry Stillday
— Michael Meuers

A FIELD GUIDE TO LOSING YOUR FRIENDS — Tyler Dunning

AWAKE IN THE WORLD V.1: A Riverfeet Press Anthology

ONE-SENTENCE JOURNAL (winner of the 2018 Montana Book Award
and the 2019 High Plains Book Award) — Chris La Tray

WILDLAND WILDFIRES: and where the wildlife go
— Randie Adams

I SEE MANY THINGS: Ninisidawenemaag, Book 1
— Erika Bailey-Johnson

LOOK AT ME — Stephany Jenkins

AWAKE IN THE WORLD V.2: A Riverfeet Press Anthology

FAMILIAR WATERS — David Stuver

BURNT TREE FORK: A Novel — J.C. Bonnell

REGARDING WILLINGNESS — Tom Harpole

LIFE LIST: POEMS — Marc Beaudin

I HEAR MANY THINGS: Ninisidawenemaag, Book 2
— Erika Bailey-Johnson

KAYAK CATE — Cate Belleveau

PAWS AND HIS BEAUTIFUL DAY — Stephany Jenkins

WITHIN THESE WOODS — Timothy Goodwin

BEYOND THE RIO GILA — Scott G. Hibbard

TEACHERS IN THE FOREST — Barry Babcock

WILTED WINGS (coming 2022) — Mike McTee

NO GOOD DAY TO DIE (coming 2022) — James Wolf

NOW AVAILABLE

TEACHERS
in the
FOREST

New Lessons from an Old World

BARRY BABCOCK

"A rewarding and enriching fusion of traditional wisdom, science and first-hand experience."
—Tristan Gooley, author of The Natural Navigator

"A rewarding and enriching fusion of traditional wisdom, science and first-hand experience." —Tristan Gooley, author of *The Natural Navigator*

Drawing from a similar lifestyle and environmental ethic as Henry D. Thoreau and Aldo Leopold, Babcock has lived more than two decades off-grid deep in the forest near the headwaters of the Mississippi River. Here he has discovered a balance in the interconnectedness of all life in the woods, and derived his sustenance from hunting, fishing, gardening, gathering wild food, providing water from a hand-pump well and minimal electricity from the sun. He befriended an Ojibwe Elder, Chi-Ma'iingan (Big Wolf), from whom he learned the Seven Grandfather Teachings (Wisdom, Love, Respect, Courage, Honesty, Humility, and Truth). In this collection, Babcock shares his love of the natural world through a unique land ethic that combines the ideology of Thoreau and Leopold, and that which he learned from Chi-Ma'iingan.

Printed in the U.S.A.

www.riverfeetpress.com

Excerpts from these pages:

"Returning to nature has been a dream present in the minds of every generation since humankind first left nature."

"I was disoriented by the idea that men should ever leave the forest."

"It occurred to me that no words by the tongue of man can express the simplicities of a quiet land, so I returned to the river."

"I miss the mountains of Wyoming, not for what they were, but for what they made me."

"If happiness required me to ignore my thoughts and questions, then I hoped to never be happy."

"This will be a test of my sanity and preparation, and I look forward to it."

"Find your own solitude to discover your hidden thoughts and think of me often, as I will you."

"The contemplative man always lives alone. Regardless of who may reside in his home, his is a solitary world."

"I believe there is a connection to wild places in all of us, and it is created by compassion and wonder for what has been lost."

"Nature has ruined me for other people."

"There is an affinity between mankind and the wild, but it is not earned fast or easy."

"My greatest hope is to forever retain the serenity of mind that was earned in the forest."

"I was lucky to be owned by a good piece of land."

"Silence is the only place where we can actual hear anything."

"Still, I found the observation of clouds and waves more enjoyable than the study of mankind."

— Hermann Hesse

THE UNPEOPLED SEASON

A Journal of Solitude and Wilderness

Daniel J. Rice

Riverfeet Press
Livingston, MT
www.riverfeetpress.com

The Unpeopled Season
A Journal of Solitude and Wilderness
Daniel J. Rice

Ten Year Anniversary Edition
Copyright 2021 © the author
Nonfiction
Memoir/Nature
ISBN-13: 978-1736089415
LCCN: 2014915326
All rights reserved
Edited by Ink Deep Editing

Title page art © Sgt. Purple
Mayfly illustration © Timothy Goodwin
Camp photos © the author
Outdoor Book Selection logo illustration © shutterstock_coz1421

First Edition information:
Copyright 2011 © the author
ISBN-13: 978-0692289464